The Prisoner

Manifesto

Nicholas J. Ely

Published by Best Self Publications.

www.morethananinmate.com

www.bestselfpublications.com

ISBN 979-8-9909504-2-9

Neither the publisher nor the author is engaged in rendering professional advice or services to the individual reader. Neither the publisher or the author shall be liable for any loss or damage allegedly arising from any information or suggestion in this book.

Acknowledgments

A Special thanks to my wife Jae from BestSelf Publications. For you I am forever grateful and will always love you.

For my family...who has been here with me through it all, never leaving my side. I love you, and am forever grateful.

For those who have made an impact on the man I've become. Yal may not even know it but in some way unique to yourself have helped shape my character, therefore, my integrity:

Tyme Bomb, Wacko (John Wack), Mezz Loc, Redd, LC, Blammo, Haze, Josh (Hoodie Hood), Bump, Coach, T-Rex, Dino, Flip, 3 times, Lil Larry, South O Joe, Zip, Ruger, Lil Mann, Lenny, Tracy (Prophet), Dre (4's), K9, Stunna, Gabe, MJ, DaVion, Shane, Wiz, Birdie, Black Foot, D-Millz, Hub Cap, Lightning, Bubba, Havek, Flick, Ozzy, Old Man, Bloody, Guerro, Silent... and the rest of the fallen angels.

Last, but not at all the least... White Boy and Lunny Tune. Through worst and through better.

Free the Guys!

Table of Contents

PART ONE

APPENDIX

Dream in Peace

"No excuses for my failures, my success – no apologies.

My only definition is absolute honesty.

You live and you learn.

I've made peace with my past.

The ones that truly care will never forget or judge you for your mistakes.

Out of sight, out of mind.

Remember me when I'm gone or forget me while I'm there.

Why share my success with me, but not struggles with me?

I don't ask nobody for nothing and I don't expect nothing from nobody.

My love will remain. "

Daelan Lamere

April 3, 1995 - June 6, 2017

Rest in Peace Lil Dreamer

Rest in Peace Q

Rest in Peace Biscuit

Rest in Peace Poe

Rest in Peace Dak

...finally free

The Inmate's Affirmation

(from the book "Serving Productive Time")

These prison walls cannot contain my heart, mind, or spirit.

I deeply regret and forgive my self for any and all wrongs committed,

and whatever damage I've done to all fellow human beings.

I forgive everyone who has misunderstood, persecuted, or abandoned me.

I am working toward the highest good for myself and others.

I am determined to leave prison a better person than when I entered-

with hope, determination, compassion, and integrity.

I will fill each day of my incarceration with love, joy, and creative

growth.

I will not allow my faith, inner strength, gentle spirit, or loving generosity

to be damaged by this or any other hostile environment.

I am not a prisoner, but a temporarily contained, worthwhile human being

waiting for my release, with lots to offer the world.

____

Your Signature

The Prisoner Manifesto

Introduction

"Prison is designed to break one's spirit and destroy one's resolve. To do this, the authorities attempt to exploit every weakness, demolish every initiative, negate all signs of individuality - all with the idea of stamping out that spark that makes each of us human and each of us who we are. Our survival depended on understanding what the authorities were attempting to do to us, and sharing that understanding with each other." - Nelson Mandela

"I am not a fan of the prison system. I am convinced that if one were charged with the responsibility of designing a system that conditions men to fail in society that person could do no better than the concept of imprisonment. In learning how-to live-in prison, the individual

simultaneously learns how to fail in society. But I've always believed that the pen is mightier than the sword, so I write." - Michael Santos

As I began writing The Prisoner Manifesto, I asked myself *"why is it necessary for me to write this script?"* If I couldn't answer why it was necessary than I wouldn't have wrote it.

This manifesto is a tool that prisoners should use to work on themselves and their lives; a magnifying glass used to discover your true self; a light to guide you on your darkest day; an inspiration to feed your creative imagination; a plea for peaceful revolution; a desire to share a part of myself with others; and a resource used to educate and agitate.

Many books for prisoners express that you need to let go of your desire for money and success by placing this desire within the realm of a "criminal mentality". Absolutely not. Although I'm personally content with the bare minimum, that is my personal philosophy born from my captor's use of deprivation as a form of punishment. If I'm content with nothing, how can they abuse me or attempt to control me? They can't. But this doesn't mean that I don't want success or material things; it just means I no longer allow these things to determine my happiness or self worth.

The Prisoner Manifesto is wrote as a mirror helping you see your true self inside of a room without a reflection. Change is a good thing, yes; without change, all life stands still. But this book is more about helping you see who and what you already are, and then guiding these qualities to the forefront of consciousness to be realized again. It doesn't require much "change in character" because most of us already have morals and are pretty smart. But it's about placing focus upon our morals and allowing them to guide your life, as well as furthering our education so that we have more opportunities in the business world.

I'm more about transforming your hustle - utilizing the same part of the brain, while being more aware of legal opportunities that are basically the same applied principles. Buy a house from the plug for $90,000 and sell it for $150,000 - pockct a $60,000 profit without stressing about the feds kicking in your door. Most people aren't even aware that there is a "plug" on houses, apartments, cars, etc.- so how can you take advantage of an opportunity that you don't even know exists? You can't, which is why a continuous education is one of the most important things in life.

So you've kind of got a grasp on the type of person I am, or how my mind is working, at least. Telling someone that they need to change is telling somebody that "who they are" as a person belongs on the other side of the playing field - the "bad" side. When I hear someone telling me I need to change, what I really hear is them saying I'm "bad", that something about me isn't right, which only angers me and makes me even more stubborn. What I'm suggesting is to allow ourselves to do what all live things in nature do... evolve. Grow. Transform. Naturally become what you were born to be and unleash your full potential. I want to see you do good, I want to see you get money and become successful, but I want to see you apply your brain and come up in a way that benefits our community, not destroys it. I've been addicted to fast money since the first time I turned $400 into $1,000 overnight and then did the same thing again the next day. Trust me, I get it. But what I'm saying is that I know we're smart enough to profit reasonably well and earn a living like the rich citizens do without having to indulge in activities that are oppressive and destructive to others. **Look,** I've had the debates over and over again about the pros and cons of hustling, how from one perspective not immoral at all but from another it's literally causing the destruction of our communities. *I'm not here to tell you what is right or wrong* (that's something each man must determine for himself), what I'm saying is you're fully capable of becoming a millionaire (even a billionaire) without giving these people the power to imprison you and without giving society a reason to believe we "deserve this". If we understand what the government has ruled as "illegal" and if we know which activities the citizens frown upon, you can only blame yourself for your predicament and cannot expect these people to ever free you.

No, don't change your desires from success to poverty- transform the way in which you intend to achieve success, aligned with a path that can ensure your freedom. The past is our roots that the tree grows from but the tree never grows if we stop evolving and educating ourselves. It stops at one height permanently til it dies, although it still had so much potential for growth and expression. Continue to water the tree of life.

Why do I feel it was necessary for me to write this book? These are the 5 reasons that I came up with:

- To clarify the principles and intentions of prisoners,

- To identify the urge, drive, or impulse that lies beneath each of our actions,

- To help others, as well as ourselves, understand our desires and why we have them,

- To educate fellow prisoners and inspire self-improvement,

- To share knowledge and experience of fellow prisoners with each other (iron sharpens iron).

"Sharing knowledge" is the price of obtaining knowledge. Give and you shall receive, sometimes tenfold. They've said that knowledge is power but this isn't necessarily true. Knowledge by itself, trapped inside one's own mind, is not power. Knowledge trapped inside one's mind may be transformative, but it is not in itself power. Instead, the application of knowledge is power. We can share knowledge with each other all day long but until we know how to apply this information to the real world, it's meaningless. We've all heard about the psychologist who has all the answers as to how to make friends and develop healthy relationships - but he himself has no friends or healthy relationships. So where lies this knowledge if the psychologist doesn't know how to apply it to his own life? Luckily for this psychologist, people will pay him money for his knowledge so he's made out okay - his knowledge transmuting to money and loneliness - but in our case, people won't be paying us for the information inside of our heads.

We need to learn how to apply what we already know, as well as integrate new information into our minds to apply when the time is right. Opportunity serves the prepared mind. "I can only show you the door.. it is you who must walk through it!" (shout out to Morpheus and The Matrix). I'm still learning how to apply my knowledge, as well as gaining new tidbits of information every day. Our journey isn't an easy one, but it is a necessary one. Necessary for us to overcome our oppression and receive our freedom... because we've always deserved it.

At the time of this writing, I've spent the last 15 years of my life in prison and I have no light at the end of the tunnel for me. I'm 33 years old and am serving a natural life sentence for a murder that they know I didn't commit but I'm forced to remain behind bars for standing upon principle. I could've been home and free 7 years ago but the thing is...*I believe in something. I believe in morals, and in values, and in principles... I believe these things so strongly inside that I'll never sacrifice or exchange them for anything, including freedom, especially not for any pieces of paper that we call money.*

My loyalty is to a code, not a person or a group, and because of this loyalty I'm considered a threat to the state and society. But, the only way any threat could possibly be conceived by this loyalty is if people don't understand the code that I'm loyal to. Rather than applauding the strength required to give up everything for your beliefs, they've assumed my loyalty to be dangerous.

There's a language barrier between the prisoners of America's *caste system* and the citizens of the *class system*. This barrier is so thick and cloudy that both ends of the spectrum can't see that we all believe in the same principles and all desire the same end; we're all saying the same thing but using different words to express our beliefs, these differences in word choice becoming a language barrier.

For example, anyone who's ever taken the time to "learn the law" in order to file their appeals and fight for their freedom all understand that the law really isn't that complicated. But it <u>appears</u> confusing, almost as if you're reading a different language, which, in a sense, you are. The words that prosecutors and lawyers speak with, the way judges structure their sentences and speak in double-negatives, the Latin terms used as names for specific proceedings - all of this has created a "language barrier" between the professionals and the common man. But upon grabbing a dictionary and breaking these words down, after reading the sentence structures out loud over and over again, we realize that we understand exactly what the fuck these people are saying! They've just covered it with what appears as mumbo jumbo in order to discourage anybody from outside of their system to interfere with their system.

It's not that the law is complicated or that we don't agree with the logic or the necessity of its placement; it's that we don't know what the fuck it's saying or what's going on at our own proceedings. We're left with the idea that we've been railroaded (you probably were) which inspires feelings of anger, hate, sadness, betrayal, helplessness...nothing positive. Now we begin to see the system and the people who are part of it (Society included) as the cause of our pain and emotions; we begin to see them as something different than us, distinct by nature -they begin to feel the same way about us as well. Funny thing is if we all agreed upon the same word play to be used while trying to express our beliefs and ideas (if we all shared the same vocabulary) most of us in the world would all believe in similar principles! A barrier within our language has caused the world to not understand the mind of a prisoner and has caused us to not understand them.

Learning the law at 24 years old changed my life forever because, not only did I learn how to file petitions and appeals, I learned about language barriers. I learned the way we speak and express ourselves can create barriers that stop us from understanding each other and if I want people to understand me then I need to learn how to express myself differently.

The loyalty I have for my code of ethics and beliefs is the same loyalty that most "good men" from society possess, and my code of ethics and beliefs are the same principles they all share amongst each other... but the words we've chosen to dress up our beliefs are different so they sound different. Therefore, a barrier. And what happens when we don't understand something? We tend to fear it. Society doesn't understand us so they fear us. Even though we came from the same society they live in, share the same society as our loved ones and people we grew up with, they don't understand the series of events that led up to us making the mistakes that landed us in prison. They can't see past our mistakes; therefore, they see us as our mistakes.

As a prison reformer, one of my goals is to help the world understand why prisons need to be reformed and why prisoners deserve freedom. Nobody will vote for any progress in prison reform if they don't believe that prisoners are worth fighting for. Long as the majority see us as the enemy to their safety and security, no "meaningful" prison reform can take effect. Meaningful in the sense that a person can go into prison ignorant and without purpose but leave educated with a new outlook on life. They've got us living in warehouses with zero intent to rehabilitate us or educate- at least from what I've seen from inside my state's prison system. Citizens scream "Be tough on crime!" because they no longer have faith that we can grow, that we can change. They no longer (and probably never did) believe that we have morals or that we're capable of developing them.

Due to these ill-conceived notions, it's now upon our own shoulders to prove that they are wrong... not through argument, but through action. Actions that each of us take within our daily lives to become better men and genuinely see the error in our ways. We need to grow and we need to educate ourselves; we need to love ourselves enough to take these first steps because no body else is gonna take them for us. Nobody is about to appear out of the blue to save us from our oppression; we are our own saviors. Being in prison places us at the forefront of this struggle.

Do you think anyone else cares about your freedom as much as you do? If you believe so, you're sadly mistaken. It's on you to earn your freedom back, on you to develop it. And I'm not using the term "Freedom" simply to mean your release from prison. Millions of people in America appear free but are not. *Only an education can free you.* What is your freedom to make a choice if your brain can't conceive of the choices? It's only an illusion, a fantasy that knowledge will shatter. In order to be liberated you must take the steps required to liberate yourself. The opening of a prison gate doesn't grant you the freedom you idealize. Most people can't even make it a year out because of the illusion they're living in. It 's time we open our eyes to see what's really going on around us.

The American Heritage dictionary defines <u>freedom</u> to mean "the capacity to act by choice rather than by determination". This definition is perfect for what I'm trying to explain. Freedom is your capacity to act by choice. But let's say for example you're released from prison tomorrow and the only thing you know is selling dope. You've never had a job and you've never seen any people become happy through working a job. All you know is that you can go grab a pack now and be straight by tomorrow. If this is all you know, then what "choice" do you really have along this pursuit of happiness? What "capacity to act by choice" is truly available to you? Because selling dope is all you know, your actions are caused by determination rather than by choice. *Determinism is when every human act is the inevitable consequence of having no other choices.* The inevitable consequence of knowing nothing other than hustling will inevitably lead to hustling which will inevitably lead to prison.

Where is the freedom in this scenario? The capacity to act by choice? How do we earn our freedom? We educate ourselves. We liberate ourselves. Stephen Covey wisely noted that the man who doesn't read is no better off than the man who doesn't know how to read. One thing that the prisons can't take away from us is our freedom to educate ourselves. We can always choose to read. Reading is an excellent means by which the mind is expanded, by which our horizons are broadened. Reading has the power to enlighten us to new choices which, in effect, broadens our capacity to act by choice rather than by determination - our freedom.

I've never believed that living outside of prison makes one "free" but until beginning my journey of liberation I couldn't understand how some people appear more free than others. Although this book is being wrote for those of us who are imprisoned, it doesn't mean that civilians aren't prisoners as well. The American Heritage dictionary has two definitions for <u>prisoner</u>: 1. person held in custody or captivity, esp.custody or captivity, esp. in a prison; 2. <u>one deprived of freedom of expression or action</u>. I prefer to apply the second definition to the term prisoner when I use it because I feel it fits those who are in prison AND those whose lack of education has caused their deprivation of freedom of expression or action. From inside of prison we are forcefully limited as to how we can act or express ourselves, but there are people outside of prison who are mentally limited as to how they can act or express themselves. *Therefore, being a prisoner applies to all whose lack of education (or limited education) has placed a ceiling upon their freedoms.*

I'm not implying that a poor education equates to dumb or stupid. Many people have the capacity to learn, the potential to develop, but have been let down by the free educational system and by our parents. We do not blame public schools, nor do we blame our parents (who were probably let down as well). Instead, we understand that we still have the capacity to learn and then we make the choice to do so. Public education is a blessing..but it's not perfect. It's an integral part of a flawed system. Many of us are in prison because of the system in place that has failed us - yet, that's not an excuse to relieve yourself from taking responsibility for your failures. Our society is doing the best it can to ensure that every child knows how to read, write, and figure out basic math. This is the lowest common denominator amongst American children. It doesn't seem like a lot but it's enough to take matters into our own hands and choose to educate ourselves.

The problem is that we believe our schools will teach us everything we need to know in order to achieve the American dream.

However, we're never told that public schools teach you just enough to be a competent worker (servant) within society and nothing more than is required to keep a job. The oil of the machine. They don't explain to us the problems inherent within public schools; they don't explain that if we truly desire freedom we'll need to educate ourselves outside of school. Because these flaws are kept from us usually until it's too late (implying our life-altering mistakes have already been made), we have been failed by the political system in place. From this point of view, I see each and every one of us as political prisoners: *being imprisoned due to a political system that has failed one as an individual and as a citizen*; not used in the sense of being imprisoned for a political crime.

After understanding what it means to be free, our predetermined choices become apparent to us. We've never had the capacity to choose anything besides what was already in place for us since birth. Depending on which family, race, or environment one was born into determines the choices that were available to each individual. And because this crucial truth has been kept from us throughout our lives and is deliberately excluded from public school curriculum, we were born with limited freedoms and have always been prisoners. Political prisoners.

A simple fix to our political system would be to teach children that our public schools are far from perfect; explain to us how children who attend private schools are receiving a far better education; enlighten us to the reality that if we desire something better for ourselves than a life of servitude, we must take matters into our own hands from a young age and educate ourselves. Our parents can't explain these concepts to us because they've only received a public education, if they even graduated. When beginning life from a point of disadvantage, the least that public schools could add to their curriculum is the teaching of how and why we're beginning at a disadvantage and what we need to do to overcome this disadvantage. No one is born equal and we're not claiming that we should be - but we should be taught that we're not born equal and that we must be more determined to break away from the chains of oppression we were born into. Most people who were born as prisoners live out their entire existence without ever understanding what has even happened and those of us who now conceptualize the conspiracy have seen it now that it's too late.

Yes... our political system has failed us and for that, we are political prisoners. But in no way does this imply that our fight is over or that we should accept our conditions. Remember: *if we don't fight for ourselves, nobody else will.* When people see us fighting for ourselves with every lick of strength from in our souls, they'll begin to fight along beside us. There's power in numbers; unity has always been a problem to those in control - and those who are in control don't want to see us with our freedom. They don't want to see us educated. They want as little competition as possible while simultaneously keeping the spotlight off of them. Therefore, they divide us and keep us focused on each other — on hurting and oppressing each other rather than allowing us to see one another as comrades who have been fighting similar struggles since birth against a flawed system.

Not only has the entire lower class been divided and turned against each other but the lines that divide prisoners from the community have become so thick that we're now viewed as a class that needs to be exterminated rather than rehabilitated. The proof of this came from the mouth of President Joe Biden back in 1996 when he was still a senator and wrote the Tough on Crime bill. He explained to congress how there is no hope for an adult criminal to be rehabilitated, arguing that measures must be enacted that push judges into handing out excessive sentences. Biden's way of thinking went that since adults can't be rehabilitated and since they obviously want criminals out of society, it was only logical to max people out and be "tough on crime". He argued that we must focus on the youth and throw away the adults. This bill was passed by former President Bill Clinton and ever since then the prison population has more than tripled. Do you understand how they view us? – as a class of people they need to rid from their communities.

Because of the divide between prisons and the community it's easier to ignore the real issue- that America has a mass incarceration problem. America has 3% of the world's human population but houses 25% of the world's inmate population. The only thing stopping the United Nations from interfering with America's abuse of the incarceration system is the fact that we're treated relatively humane. But this doesn't make it acceptable that they're getting away with it. Those numbers are drastically out of proportion.

As the ones who are suffering, we need to join hands with each other and transform the way that we're living. If we don't, they'll never let us out of these places. And that's a fact. If we can't show the world that we're worthy of freedom, that we're mature enough to maintain the responsibility of it, they will lose us in these prisons and many of us will die in here. I'm already on the path of dying behind these walls (having been sentenced to natural life) and if something doesn't change - if we don't change as a people - millions of other people just like me and you will die back here too. Things only get worst. It hasn't been getting any better in my world- but we as a people haven't been showing any progress. either. We already know where hustling and violence gets us. Let's try to see where education and proactive behavior gets us.

I'm writing this book as a manifesto because that's what it is. The American Heritage dictionary defines <u>manifesto</u> as *"a public declaration of principles or intentions, esp. political ones"*. Herein I'm declaring to the public that *we are not who or what you think we are*, that we are more than the stereotype you imagine us to be, and that there is potential back here that we refuse to let be wasted. I will lay out what our principles are, as prisoners, and what our intentions are as a class of people. I will explain which political system best fits our principles and our intentions.

Inside are the principles and intentions of those who have been deprived their freedom of expression or action. I'll assist us in expressing what it is we all truly desire, even if some of us have yet to understand what it is that determines all of our actions.

This is The Prisoner Manifesto... a guide to furthering our education and mending the bridge between us and the community.

"If we don't write our own endings, we hand our pens over to the legislators, owners of privatized prisons, and propagators of the lies behind mass incarceration. Write about prison because there are more people in prisons in America than populate some small countries. Because your experiences are the experiences of countless others. Write because there is truth in our stories that cannot, must not be denied: the separation from our families, the toll on our loved ones, all the wasted time, the warehousing of our bodies, and our fruitless efforts to prevail against a

flawed reality of incarceration. That is the story we dare everyone to acknowledge. And only we can tell it as it truly is." - Derek R. Trumbe St.

PART ONE

What is integrity?

A. Integrity is doing the right thing when nobody's looking.

Q. Are you a leader or a follower?

A. I'm a leader.

Q. What's the difference?

A. Think for myself.

Q. Do you have confidence?

A. Yes.

Q. What's confidence?

A. Believe in myself.

-Nipsey Hussle

<u>Integrity</u>

We've heard the word all throughout our lives but have never really had a clear understanding of what it actually means. What does it mean to be a man of integrity and why is it important?

The American Heritage dictionary defines integrity as *"steadfast adherence to a strict moral or ethical code"* derived from the Latin integer, or "whole".

This definition explains the term efficiently but now we must consider *"steadfast adherence"* and what that entails, as well as <u>which/what</u> "strict moral or ethical code" does one adhere to.

Integrity is, basically, your loyalty to a belief system. *"Steadfast adherence"* is one's loyalty and a *"strict moral or ethical code"* is one's belief system. To be a man of integrity you must have a clear understanding of what it is that you believe in and the principles/values that you stand on. We all know people who talk a good game but their actions never match their words - this is the opposite of integrity. Integrity is doing the right thing even when no one is looking. What does it say about someone who "does the right thing even when no one is looking"? It means the decisions someone chooses to make and act upon rest at the core of a person's character and belief system; they're not choices made inspired by social acceptance or fear of ridicule. They are part of the person's organizing principles, proven by the fact the decision was made and stood upon "even when no one is looking".

But, this still doesn't clearly define what is said about a man of integrity. A man, who does the right thing - yes. But, what's the right thing? What is right? What one labels as "right" is subjective to the individual. It's not some clear, objective concept set in stone for everybody to follow. Because of this - and for your own mental clarity - it is important to identify what is right <u>to you</u> and what is <u>right to the person whose integrity is in question</u>. Do you share the same core beliefs as this person, or do you differ on what you believe is right? Without an objective or collective set of virtues and principles that everyone agrees on, the question of integrity becomes open-ended. Because of this, it's imperative to develop a personal system of integrity (or adapt one from religion, philosophy, or society), express it to the world in some way, personifying your system and give a public declaration that *"I am a man of integrity and this is what I believe in"*. This is what religious medallions, brand names, and tattoos are supposed to symbolize to the world.

Integrity is integrating one's character into a proper whole; maintaining control over one's vices while applying virtues.

Integrity turns scribbles into a circle. Completeness, harmony, wholeness. A solid character inspires peace of mind - Peace of mind comes when your life is in harmony with principles and values.

"The art of a great soldier is not in his ability to fight but in his ability to maintain his dignity, pride, and self-respect, and, most of all, his humanity in his darkest hour!" - Albert Wood fox

What makes up our integrity makes up the roots from which our character grows, from which our vision blossoms and our dreams are manifested. Without Roots, nothing can grow. But without a seed to bury in the soil and bring to life, no roots can sprout. We are not born with integrity; it is something we must discover and develop throughout our lives. It is an "active" quality, one you must actively nurture and allow to become. It will not come to those who do not plant the seed and water it daily.

As a way of living, integrity requires focus and self-discipline, an understanding of the bigger picture.

In the beginning it takes time to integrate a newly learned "code of conduct" into daily life. You may have an idealistic passion of progress but still have an undeveloped control of emotions that lead to mistakes in action. The goal is to always return to the principles and values you've come to believe in, eventually reaching the point where one is of integrity. This journey of becoming will lead you away from the life of a criminal.

Your own personal conduct (the way you behave) is more important than the things you say. Hypocritical behavior - saying one thing but doing another - is a deduction from one's integrity. Following through in action with the things you say develops trust from others, like a moral credit.

Manifest integrity by being loyal to those who are not present. By this you'll earn the trust of those who are present. They'll see that you are a man of strong character, possessing a backbone that doesn't conform to societal pressures.

"There can be no friendship without confidence, and no confidence without integrity." - Samuel Johnson

Keeping promises and fulfilling expectations is a symbol of one's integrity as it shows you place value on your word and on the word of others. Conform reality to your words; if you don't mean it, don't say it.

"Integrity is a higher value than loyalty. Or better put, integrity is the highest form of loyalty. Integrity means being integrated or centered on principles not on people, organizations, or even family. You will find that the root of most issues that people are dealing with is "is it popular (acceptable, political), or is it right?" When we prioritize being loyal to a person or group over doing what we feel to be right, we lose integrity. We may temporarily gain popularity or build loyalty, but, down stream, this loss of integrity will undermine even those relationships.... Over time, integrity produces. loyalty. If you attempt to reverse them and go for loyalty first, you will find yourself temporizing and compromising integrity."
-Stephen Covey

Now that we've covered pretty thoroughly what integrity is, let us discuss why integrity is important. While working on this chapter, I had to ask myself" "Is integrity even important or necessary to a person who has no desire to interact with, or become successful in, the social realm?" The answer to this question, put simply, is No. If you have no desire to be a part of your society or environment, if you care not about receiving respect from others or interacting with any of the voices outside of your head, then integrity is not important at all. But for he who chooses to interact with others and desires success in any way, integrity is everything. It's your "welcome" pass; it's the key through the doorway of entry. It is what allows others to let down their guards around you and be willing to network.

Integrity is so important in human affairs because at the end of the day, when it all comes down to it... *a person can never truly know another person*. No matter how hard we try or how much we truly desire to, it is impossible to know exactly what's going on inside someone else's head. It is impossible to know exactly what's going through someone's mind, impossible to know exactly how another person views the world or is feeling about things in any given moment, as each of our subjective universes differ from one another's. We each live inside our own little world that nobody else can share with us, making it almost impossible to know what the next person may do. This truth could leave us with the ever-present danger of dealing with strangers (remember lessons learned from Big Brother) making it impossible to trust each other in the social realm.

Because of this "wild card" (the differences between us) the one and only way we can know a person's truth is through their integrity. Habitual actions over time and one's loyalty to a set of basic principles, values and virtues act as a symbol expressed to the social realm that *"I am a person worthy of trust. I am a person worthy of working with, worthy of building with. I am a safe zone"*. Without integrity one is simply a stranger who cannot be relied upon and can never be known. A wild card.

Integrity acts as a microscope into the layers of one's core, allowing another person to see exactly what is needed for them to make a decision as to whether or not they can trust you. If we ever want to be accepted into our society again, if we ever want to receive the freedom we so desperately desire, we need our society to trust that they know what to expect from us. When people can trust that we're not "wild cards" let loose amongst their neighborhoods and loved ones but, instead, are humans whose actions can be predicted due to our integrity... what need is there to further our imprisonment?

Freedom requires responsibility. Without responsibility, one does not deserve freedom. Our integrity is the active proof to the world that we are responsible and in total control of our behaviors, that we are no longer a threat to ourselves or others. Allow others to see that we are determined to become better people even while realizing that we live in a world where "being better" sometimes means nothing. This speaks to your strength in character, the fullness of your soul.

The best thing about it is that integrity is a choice. Between stimulus and a response, we have the freedom to choose... Choosing the proper action becomes more simple once we know the proper action... and after gaining control of emotional influences. This begins with education and discipline, two things that nobody is born with.

Every prisoner intends to be a man of integrity. It helps to actually understand what integrity is and why it is important.

Give Me Liberty, or Give Me Death!
(a passage)

"My manner of thinking, so you say, cannot be approved. Do you suppose I care? A poor fool indeed is he who adopts a manner of thinking for others! My manner of thinking stems from my considered reflections; it holds with my existence, with the way I am made. It is not in my power to alter it; and were it, I'd not do so. This manner of thinking you find fault with is my sole consolation in life; it alleviates my sufferings in prison, it composes all my pleasures in the world outside, it is dearer to me than life itself. Not my manner of thinking but the manner of thinking of others has been the source of my unhappiness. The reasoning man who scorns the prejudices of simpletons necessarily becomes the enemy of simpletons; he must expect as much, and laugh at the inevitable. A traveler journeys along a fine road. It has been strewn with traps. He falls into one. Do you say it is the traveler's fault, or that of the scoundrel who lays the traps? If then, as you tell me, they are willing to restore my liberty if I am willing to pay for it by the sacrifice of my principles or my tastes, we may bid one another an eternal adieu, for rather than part with those, I would sacrifice a thousand lives and a thousand liberties, if I had them. These principles and these tastes, I am their fanatic adherent; and fanaticism in me is the product of the persecutions I have endured from my tyrants. The longer they continue

their vexations, the deeper they root my principles in my heart, and openly declare that no one need ever talk to me of liberty/ if it is offered only in return of their destruction."

The Marquis de Sade - In a letter to his wife

Virtues, Vices, and Principles

There's a basic list of principles that is universal amongst all prisoners, at every prison (at least in America). Upon entering one of our prisons you should know we all stand for and are supposed to abide by these principles:

1) No snitchin'

2) No stealing

3) Mind your own business

4) Pay your bills

5) Respect people's space

6) Don't call people out of their name

If you can abide by these simple rules, most of the time you'll end up okay in here. There are always a few exceptions wherever you go, but this list is universal for the most part. It comes down to respect – respect for the next man and respect for yourself.

Abiding by these same behaviors in society would do us all well, if only we all had enough self-discipline and the desire to do so. Most people in prison abide by these principles because there's severe consequences for being out of bounds. Not all prisoners actually believe in these policies personally. But what if they did? Wouldn't these principles be some pretty basic guidelines to freedom (which requires responsibility)? To staying out of trouble? If you don't steal (or rob) and you respect people's space, that alone would release hundreds of thousands of people out of prison. If you mind your own business and don't disrespect people, you won't have any trouble from others in society. If you pay your bills, your credit line increases and you can take out bigger loans to use for a small business or mortgage. And, finally, don't cooperate with the government to oppress any individuals (snitchin'). Don't involve yourself in shit that doesn't pertain to you. If you're scared to come back to prison (as you always should be) - don't break the law!' Simple as that.

For every action there is a reaction; you reap what you sow. Most problems within our lives have generated from earlier decisions we made.

Honest self-reflection will prove that there were other paths we could've taken, other choices we could've made, but somewhere along the chain of events we fucked up - and now we're in prison. If we don't want to come back to prison again (or the hole) we need to be conscious of how every one of our actions has a reaction throughout the universe. You can never believe that your choices don't matter or that they have no effect in the universe. Everything you do matters. The choice between watching TV for an hour this morning or reading a book for an hour can determine two separate paths your life will take... from such a simple, small decision.

"Sometimes when I consider what tremendous consequences come from little things... I am tempted to think.... there are no little things."
- Bruce Barton

There are no "little things". Every choice you make has tremendous consequences. Whether you're conscious of the consequences is irrelevant. The ripple has still been sent into the universe. Every action has a reaction.

"Principles are deep, fundamental truths, classic truths, generic common denominators. They are tightly interwoven threads running with exactness, consistency, beauty, and strength through the fabric of life...Principles always have natural consequences attached to them. They

are positive when we live in harmony with the principles. There are negative consequences when we ignore them. But because the principles apply to everyone, whether or not they are aware, this limitation is universal. And the more we know of correct principles, the greater is our personal freedom." - Stephen Covey

And this is what a principle is... the natural laws that determine how every action will be reacted to. Abide by principles and you go with nature's flow. Violate her principles and you will witness a cruelty unimagined.

Principles are important to know and to follow. The Egyptian gods (the neteru) represented universal principles. You were blessed by following them or cursed by going against or ignoring them. Reactions are so real that entire religions were invented (and followed) with the intent of ensuring the masses would abide by universal principles. Using authority from a higher power, prophets and priests taught people how to live on principles, threatening them with eternal punishment for refusing to do so.

This method to keep the masses in line worked for thousands of years, but what happens when the masses stop believing the myths? Where does the authority now come from that dictates how they behave? Here's the thing.... universal principles are in effect whether you believe in them or not. Natural laws have nothing to do with faith - they require understanding to receive the benefits.

But without a religion or some authority teaching these principles or providing appropriate guidelines to follow, many of us grew up lost. Confused as to our purpose, we allow our animal instinct to guide us - and these actions have severe consequences within a civilization of "domesticated" animals, i.e. humans. They're not putting up with your "wild side" any longer and, as we now know, they've got a place for us!

We've got to turn to ourselves for that inner authority, depend on ourselves to learn about principles and virtues. In prison there's usually an inmate who has power over others (the head of the car, or whatever) and this authority serves to show people in here how they must act... or else. And this is where the 6 universal principles that prisoners abide by come into play. But as it was with the "unthinking followers" of religions of past, what happens when they no longer have that authority over their life? What happens when they get out of prison and no longer have the threat of being "taken out" if they violate? Well... they tend to go back to their old ways and begin violating these principles again. This is what happens with those who don't genuinely believe in these principles while inside but only follow them for their own personal safety out of fear of punishment (or war). They have no "inner authority" guiding their life or their actions, only the animal instincts.

Those who follow any authority outside of themselves will always come back to prison. You must believe in these things you live your life by ... or at least understand their benefits enough to train yourself to abide by them, inside and out. Integrity is doing the right thing even when no one's looking. The prisoners who don't have an inner authority won't follow all of these principles when no one's looking. And there, my friend, lies the problem. A problem of hypocritical behavior - when one's actions do not reflect the thoughts/feelings going through one's head. This is the opposite of integrity. Here lies the crack in the foundation of those who you've known for decades to be solid-real and then one day break under pressure. It may seem as if their behavior came "out of nowhere" but, in truth, this person had been struggling to balance his inner thoughts/feelings with his outer actions. His belief in virtues and principles was a façade and the mask fell off. Integrity is only integrity when the individual truly believes the moral code of ethics he is loyal to. If these beliefs aren't genuine, the trained eye will be able to peep specific signs in one's behavior or words that indicate "danger" - that a person is faking it and needs to be watched from a distance.

Again, I say the "trained eye" because these signs are usually subtle (or come as Freudian slips) and those who are new to the game will overlook the behavior. The man of integrity understands how imperative it is that we only deal with other men of integrity, and life sometimes feels like a continuous process of eliminating those who don't make the cut. Men of integrity recognize the signs of integrity in other men. Real recognize Real. Real eyes Realize. There's always gonna be the snakes in the grass, and we know this – therefore we train the eye to see what's going through the mind of the person behind the actions. Actions speak a language of their own, just as integrity has a language of its own. It's on you to develop the eyes of understanding.

"Just cuz he say he gon ride, don't mean he loyal dawg. It's Cain and Abel again, forgive us Father God." – Boosie

As children it was hard for us to determine between what was "right and wrong" unless we had someone telling us which is what. We weren't born with some objective list of "right" virtues that the world agreed to and follows.

I grew up making decisions based on what I felt was right at that moment. And I made a lot of mistakes. If any one were to ask me what virtues I value, or what code of ethics was my guiding force, I'd have had no idea how to answer. "What virtues do I value?" I couldn't have told you what a virtue was at the time. Now I know that a virtue is a positive character trait, one that pushes you forward in life (as opposed to a vice, which is something that holds you back).

I never had anybody sit me down and tell me "These are specific virtues that you should live your life by". Even if I'd have never listened as a child or was too young to comprehend, it still would have been something I'd benefit from as I matured because this list of virtues would have been programmed into the core of who I am, resting within my mind and guiding me subconsciously. Lucky for me, I had a mother and father in my life (divorced) who I could watch and absorb a few "do's /don'ts" - but what every household needs to have hanging up in their living room is a clear list of virtues that the family has chosen to value and live by. Like a constitution, this gives a precise understanding of what is expected from the individuals within the household and can be tools that guide one's behavior. Having a list of virtues memorized and at the forefront of consciousness makes it harder for one to give into vice or make bad decisions.

Integrity is having a list of virtues that you live up to within your daily life. Knowing exactly what it is that you actually value (and why it is that you value it) makes it so much simpler to remain loyal to it. If you want to raise your children with integrity, the first step should be to develop a list of virtues that you believe will benefit them throughout life. Then make it physical. Give it a presence and life of its own by printing the list onto computer paper (maybe with a nice border around it) and title it "(Family's last name) Virtues of Integrity". Place it in a frame and hang it up on a wall in the living room area that way every single day of your children's life they wake up and see this list of positive traits that their family values. It brings a sense of unity, energy, essence, and life to the family name - what it means to be a "family name".

You should do the same thing inside your prison cell. If you don't have anyone who will print a list of your personal virtues (with a brief definition of each one) and send it to you in the mail, write them out clearly on a piece of paper yourself and tape it to your wall. It all starts with ourselves. We can't tell somebody to live a certain way when we ourselves live differently. If you have bad hand writing, have a friend with good hand writing (or pay an artist) to write this list out for you - then hang it up on the wall in your prison cell for you to see every morning, day, and night. Other prisoners (and maybe even guards) will respect this when they see it.

But first things first... *you must have a list of virtues you value!* It took me years of reflecting on who I was as a man, searching my soul to discover what it is I truly care about in life, before I was able to manifest my list of virtues that make up my integrity. We all may know one or two virtues off the top of our head that we value but what I'm referring to is a list that encircles every action of your entire life, something that leaves no "loose ends" or open questions as to how one should act or who one is inside. The list should be extensive but not repetitive. Many of the virtues I'd heard before but had no idea what they even meant... which is why a brief definition of each virtue should be provided within your new family constitution.

Just as a solid constitution is the glue that holds a country together, your personal constitution is the glue that can hold your family together... and even yourself. Make the word "family" imply something more than sharing blood lines. A family could share in beliefs, as well. "Blood makes us related, Loyalty makes us family". Yes - but, loyalty to what? Add something to the family name that gives one something to be loyal to...above all else. Add depth to what it means to be part of this family or tribe or group. This will create generational ties and inspire destinies. Before an empire can be constructed there must be a constitution that guides all action. Every building must be built upon a solid structure. If you want your pyramid to reach the stars, how broad must be your foundation? Integrity is the first step.

I'm sharing my list of virtues that I've discovered to accurately represent my integrity, who I am as a man, and what I'd like my family to be built upon. Feel free to use a few of them, or, if this list of virtues hits home for you, go ahead and adopt it in its entirety. It's a tool to one's growth.

<u>12 Virtues of Integrity</u>

1) Reliability (worthy of trust and responsibility, good credit)

2) Humility (humble, not allowing pride to be counterproductive)

3) Prudence (wise in practical matters, foresight and good judgment)

4) Fortitude (strength of mind to endure pain or adversity with courage).

5) Resilience (recovering from misfortune without losing hope)

6) Patience (enduring pain or difficulty with calmness; understanding; tolerant)

7) Studiousness (living with purpose, inclined toward diligent study)

8) Temperance (moderation and self-restraint)

9) Justice (being honorable and fair, righteousness)

10) Gratitude (being thankful for life and all you have received)

11) Progress (transcendence, development, moving forward, creative improvement)

12) Tranquility (peace of mind, calm; free from agitation).

Virtues are qualities of being that will lead us to an increase of positivity in character. They can be developed by watching the actions of those who possess and emulate them. Virtuous people are usually noticeable by the quality of their lives, their attitude, and their success. Virtues push you forward in life so most virtuous people end up ahead even after starting from behind.

On the other hand, a <u>vice</u> is a habit or quality of mind that holds us back from our self-determined goals. One must analyze the behaviors that support a vice and eliminate them. But, like virtues, you must discover what you see a vice to be after being completely honest with yourself. Some people can handle certain activities better than others. The test is to compare these behaviors to self-determined goals. Do these behaviors assist you in attaining your goals (in reality) or do they hold you back? This is how you can determine your vices.

I've provided an objective list of vices that can't assist anybody in reaching their goals. Eliminate these traits from your behaviors and character.

<u>12 Vices</u>
1) Resentment (feeling bitter towards life and people)

2) Complacency (settling for a situation or relationship without completeness)

3) Stupidity (a lack of education)

4) Avarice (extremely greedy, being controlled by money)

5) Rashness (making bold decisions not backed by impulsion)

6) Solipsism (believing that everyone thinks how you think)

7) Wantonness (unrestrained behavior, a lack of self-control)

8) Indolence (laziness, undetermined)

9) Lack of Perspective (not capable of considering other points of view)

10) Despair (the loss of hope).

11) Self-Deceit (lying to yourself)

12) Addiction (physically or mentally dependent on something)

Avoid these vices in their entirety and you will grow in character, as well as move faster towards achieving your goals. Men of integrity are honest with themselves about what problems they face and make a continuous effort to overcome these challenges. Vices aren't necessarily "bad"; remember that these things are subjective. For example, I'm "addicted" to coffee but I don't view it as a vice because I can afford coffee and its consumption actually assists me in achieving my goals. So you see, this isn't a list of "cookie cutter" behaviors to eliminate but a guide to help raise awareness as to what your own vices actually are and to develop your own inner authority.

Because we were never taught these things growing up and because we may not even know where to begin learning these things, I've found it helpful to use other people's list of principles and virtues as I travel my journey. Through experimenting with behaviors and judging the outcomes I now know what works for me and what I believe to be true - at least for my life. But still I leave room for growth, always until I die, as a "continuous education" has become one of the factors that guide my existence. Morals and principles will always be true in my world.

Here's a list of 12 principles that I have found to develop wisdom in all their individuality.

12 Principles to obtain Wisdom

1) Take care of yourself - physically, emotionally, spiritually

2) Live your life out of Vision, not out of circumstance

3) Develop a strong bullshit detector

4) Don't let your ego fool you

5) Be reticent in public

6) Focus on Healing, NOT on what is divisive

7) Work regularly to increase your willpower

8) React prudently to the vicissitudes of life

9) Treat cheating like it's treason

10) Don't let customs or tradition overrule your own good judgment

11) Always remind children of their importance to society

12) Be the change you want to see in the world

The American Heritage dictionary defines these words to mean:

Ego - 1. the self, esp. as distinct from all others... 3. An exaggerated sense of self-importance; conceit.

Reticent - 1. Inclined to keep one's personal affairs to oneself. 2. Restrained or reserved.

Divisive-creating dissension or discord. (Dissension - difference of opinion)

Prudent - wise in practical matters; exercising good judgment.

Vicissitude - 1. A change or variation. 2. A usu. unforeseen change in circumstance or experience that affects one's life.

Treason - The betrayal of one's country, esp. by aiding an enemy.

Agents of Change

"Understand that fascism is already here, that people are already dying who could be saved, that generations more will die or live poor butchered half-lives if you fail to act. Do what must be done, discover your humanity and your love in revolution.... Join us, give up your life for the people." - George Jackson (killed in prison by guards)

How do we become agents of change? How do we play our role at the forefront of incarceration? The first thing you can begin to do is <u>alter the way you see your "time"</u>. The way we spend our days is a reflection of the value we place on time - man's most valuable natural resource. Sitting around all day doing nothing is similar to turning on the faucet to let water run for no reason - the difference is that our time is going to run out someday (whereas in America you'll just run up an expensive water bill). Being in prison gives us time without distractions - something that people in society don't have. People out there have jobs, go to school, raise kids, have cell phones and social media, sexual partners – all these things that distract them and fill up their time. They have responsibilities and entertainment- two things we really don't have. Our rent is paid (there is no rent), food and showers are provided, toilet paper, etc. We're fine for the most part. Making the choice to spend your time wisely is the first step to becoming an agent of change.

"The way you spend your time is a result of the way you see your time and the way you really see your priorities." - Stephen Covey

After you've altered the way you see your time (by having placed more value on it than money), you must <u>create a routine that pushes you toward your goals AND STICK TO IT!</u>

"We are what we repeatedly do.

Excellence, then, is not an act, but a habit." – Aristotle

Now that you value your time, sit down and write a schedule or agenda that you feel capable of committing to. Be realistic with yourself and don't start off with any drastic changes. The first few days of your new routine will either be difficult at first to maintain, OR, the opposite- easy due to your energetic excitement of starting something new. The problem with this "energetic excitement" is that it wears off quickly. Without willpower, one will fall back into his old habits very quickly. It's better to expect and plan for it to be a bit difficult, a bit different. Thing is, human beings are masters of adapting and adjusting. We usually adapt due to an outside force that makes us, but willpower is the inside force (that inner authority) that makes us abide by a new routine and develop different habits.

"Willpower is but the unflinching purpose to carry a task you set for yourself to fulfillment. If I set for myself a task, be it ever so trifling, I shall see it through. How else shall I have confidence in myself to do important things?" - The Richest Man in Babylon

It's imperative for one's growth and integrity to follow through with an activity once you've told yourself (or someone else) that you're going to do it. Therefore, make your daily routine reasonable and applicable to your daily life. If after the first few days you feel you've overstepped your own expectations, don't blame yourself or feel shame - sit down and edit your routine. It's not a big deal. However, quitting all together is a problem. We don't quit. Developing a routine (healthy habits) is a small personal victory that prepares you for the larger victories. Without these small preparations we cannot win the battle. And what are we fighting for? Our freedom. The stakes couldn't be higher. It's like learning how to play chess; first you learn how the pieces move, then comes the strategies. We must know how to move before we can ever win.

A life of integrity is when our daily habits reflect our deepest values. What is said about your values and priorities if your entire day is spent watching TV or playing spades? For one thing, it shows you enjoy turning on the water faucet and walking away. Who wants to fight for people who waste natural resources? Your daily routine is the first step in learning how to exploit your time, to make it as abundant and rich as possible.

Where do you start with this new routine? First, make a list of all the daily activities that you have no choice in the matter of "when" they must be done, such as: work, school, dining, yard, religion, recreation, clubs, lock down, etc. Mark these activities down on paper so you can see how much free time you have available. Once this is done, determine a reasonable time that you will wake up each morning and go to sleep each night. There can be NO sleeping in all morning and staying up all night; this is detrimental to any kind of success (unless you actually work the night shift). No matter what, every single morning without failure, I wake up and get out of bed at 5:30 AM. The very first things I do before ever speaking a word to anybody is brush my teeth, wash my face, and make my bed.

Always make your bed first thing in the morning. It's proven to make you more proactive throughout the day and less depressed.

After I've done these things, I take a few moments to give myself a "positive affirmation" while looking in the mirror, I read my passage from scripture and Robert Greene's "The Daily Laws", then I check my emails.

Once all of this is done, it's about 6 AM which is when I begin my reading and/or writing. My entire mornings are dedicated to reading/writing. I play my "rain/thunderstorm" playlist in my ears to block out my environment and help me focus. It's never good to listen to music with lyrics while reading or writing - someone else's words take away from the focus of your own thoughts.

At around 10 AM I may take a brief nap or walk around for 30 minutes depending on my mood. Then I'll spend some time replying to emails or self-reflecting.

Lunch comes around this time which I'll put to the side til later because around noon is time for my exercise routine. I stretch and mentally prepare myself for the routine ahead. Complete the exercise routine, then I'll eat my food as well as some protein, and relax my body for a bit before taking a shower. This all takes approximately two-hours.

I don't have a job or school or programs/clubs (as I'm housed in a maximum - security unit of controlled movement wherein we only get three-hours out-of-cell per day) so I have more free time on my hands than most prisoners. But, the one thing I never do throughout the day to fill up my time is watch the television. That's a sin to my personal faith. When making your new routine, incorporate "no television until after 6pm throughout the week" for any reason. The TV is a vice (especially the news/media), a weapon used against us (under the guise of a privilege). It has the power to cause disunity and disharmony. When we see the TV as a privilege, we're efficiently brainwashed by civilization (Hollywood, in particular). This affects all of us; it's not a shot against anybody. I'm saying this to recognize the fact and take your mind back for yourself. It's amazing how free your mind feels and how differently you'll think after going a year without watching television. It's like being unplugged from The Matrix and experiencing reality for the first time - painful at first but once you've adjusted, you'll never wanna go back to that world of horrors. No TV until after 6 PM - make it sacred. Utilize your days wisely.

"We can't watch television for three hours, then read the Bible for three minutes and expect to grow.... If you're serious about defeating temptation you must manage your mind and monitor your media intake.....Don't allow trash into your mind indiscriminately." - Rick Warren

The same principle that applies to spirituality applies to education and personal growth. It's common sense, everybody. Eliminate the box.

Finally, to end your routine, set a reasonable bedtime for yourself to sleep around 9 pm each night in order to receive adequate rest and prepare yourself for the next morning. Each day you start over.

Everyone's routine will be different as they are meant for the individual but one thing that every routine must include and never neglect is your civil duty to educate yourself. This is the next step we take - and is the most important step to achieving freedom. In prison, the world becomes open to those who read. This is why it is such an important step to overcoming our oppression. Every social revolutionary has became who they were through the power of reading.

"People don't realize how a man's whole life can be changed by one book." – Malcolm X

While serving his prison bid, Malcolm X made the decision to read any book he could get his hands on- and it transformed him! Look who he became from behind the walls and look at the effect he had on the world- which all started with making the decision to arm himself with knowledge. He who chooses not to seek knowledge is the boy who chooses not to become a man. Allow your continuous education to become your faith!

"Only the educated are free". – Epictetus

One thing that all successful people have in common is that they never stop learning; they never reach a point where they're content with their knowledge, understanding that knowledge is the key to opportunity.

Another beautiful fact about choosing to educate yourself is that the prison administration can't stop it. The one weapon we have against them is the one thing they can't deny us - our first amendment right to read (as well as to religion). Even in the hole they must allow you reading material. In my journey, the years I spent in solitary confinement have been the most transformative years of my life. Alone in my cell, zero distractions - nothing but books, paper, a pen, my mind and some time. Solitary confinement is illegally used as a punishment with the specific intent to break a prisoner. Ever heard the phrase "it'll make you or break you?" It's our responsibility to NOT let it break us.

In his book called "Solitary," Albert Woodfox, a prisoner who spent over 40 years in solitary confinement, mastered this concept:

"By the time I was 40 I saw how I had transformed my cell, which was supposed to be a confined space of destruction and punishment, into something positive. I used that space to educate myself, I used that space to build strong moral character, I used that space to develop principles and code of conduct, I used that space for everything other than what my captors intended it to be."

At another time, Woodfox said *"I became something they didn't want or expect - self-educated. I could lose myself in a book. Reading was a bright spot for me. Reading was my salvation."*

All of us can, and must, transform our cage into a place of education and positivity. And nothing but our own mind can stop us from doing so.

Nelson Mandela wrote that the challenge for every prisoner is *"how to survive prison intact, how to emerge from prison undiminished, how to conserve and even replenish one's beliefs."* Nelson Mandella served

27 years incarcerated as a political prisoner before he became president of

South Africa and revolutionized his country. Do you think he ever stopped

educating himself? Absolutely not.

One can educate themselves in many ways; there are several

different types of education. For example, personal experience and one's

own trial and error are the most efficient forms. Unfortunately, our personal

experiences are limited as prisoners and there are only so many things that

we can do while incarcerated. Our education will come from reading, or

classes and clubs like 7 Habits and Toastmasters, as well as learning

ourselves - who and what we truly are. You can do a lot of soul-searching

while reading, as well as travel through the minds of others from our

generation and into the ancient past.

Prisons set out to reduce our value as human beings in order to

break our will. The oppressed will always believe the worst about

themselves. We must educate ourselves, develop a sense of confidence and

inner security. We must stop seeing each other and society as our enemy

because if we can't come together, we'll never be able to resist the

downward pull of negativity. We deserve better than what we're getting.

The problem has never been us. The problem is the system. Put good people

in a bad system, you end up with bad results. Education is our salvation.

There's only so much that we ourselves can do from behind the walls. We become limited as to how far we can go, how much we can accomplish, without being forced to depend on others. Because I have been let down so frequently by so many different people, I began to place the highest value on my personal independence. I told myself that I didn't need anybody and I set out to prove it. Unreliable people gave me the desire to become a sovereign. But, over time I kept running into the same barriers that all prisoners face… needing help from other people. We can't do this on our own. And we don't need to. If we want our efforts to reach beyond these walls and affect society in a meaningful way, the next step to becoming an agent of change is to <u>Network</u>. Seek reliable people-people of integrity - inside of prison and out.

It's incredibly important to be independent but it's even more important to become interdependent. Interdependence is understanding the value in a master mind group, believing two minds are better than one, and being able to work together in a network to accomplish goals that couldn't be accomplished by yourself. Thing is, only independent people - men of integrity - can choose to be interdependent. Dependent people don't have the character to do so. They'd rather "use" somebody than work with them. Independent people add value to their network circle.

"Life is, by nature, highly interdependent. To try to achieve maximum effectiveness through independence is like trying to play tennis with a golf club - the tool is not suited to the reality.

Interdependence is a far more mature, more advanced concept. If I am physically interdependent, I am self-reliant and capable, but I also realize that you and I working together can accomplish far more than, even at my best, I could accomplish alone. If I am emotionally interdependent, I derive a great sense of worth within myself, but I also recognize the need for love, for giving, and for receiving love from others. If I am intellectually interdependent, I realize that I need the best thinking of other people to join with my own." - Stephen Covey

In society, a sense of interdependency is more important than independency. The outlook that we are all responsible people but we need each other to keep this whole thing operating. And there's nothing wrong with that. The right group of people in sync can move mountains. It's hard for people who have held on to their independence for so long to relinquish some of this control to others but it must be done. Our goal is to work with society, to work with people, to become part of the people again. If we can't trust them, why would they trust us?

Of course, we have to be particular about who we choose to trust and build a team with. I mean, most of us have become independent after trusting the wrong people and being let down. It's very important to network with those of integrity. In our position, reliability must be valued more than their talent. I don't care if you're the most talented person...if I can't depend on you when it counts, then your talent will never count. Choose reliability over talent when determining who you'd like to network with.

As we reach out to people in the free world we always need to remember to respect people's boundaries. Build relationships that have lines that shouldn't be crossed.... and don't cross them. I've had this problem in the past and ultimately ruined the chances to network with people because I didn't respect boundaries. There was a point when I was seriously questioning whether I could "just be friends" with a woman and if being friends with a member of the sex I'm attracted to was even possible. I had to ask my cellie one day, "From in here, do you think it's possible to talk to a female as a friend and nothing more?" He started laughing and answered, "Hell no. It might be all good for awhile but eventually Ima be laying here one night, Ima be horny because I'm in prison and Ima end up saying something to her that I probably shouldn't say. And then the friendship is over. I've did it over and over, even when I tell myself not to." I started laughing with him because it's something I relate to but had never heard spoken out loud before.

That answer helped me learn something about us, as prisoners. If we want to build meaningful relationships with people and develop efficient networking opportunities, we must respect the boundaries that are in place. That goes for out in society as well. And I don't wanna hear "I didn't know what the boundaries were in the relationship!" That's no excuse. You know goddam well what the boundaries are but sometimes that animal nature gets a hold of us and chemically alters our way of thinking. We're sexually repressed (having no conjugal visit opportunities) so sometimes I'd like to say "it's not our fault" ... but, it is. Between every stimulus and response lies the freedom to choose. We have to maintain control over ourselves in our moments of weakness because one mistake can damage or end the relationship. We have bigger goals we're trying to accomplish-remember your goals while battling temptation. Now that I "know myself" and the struggles I face daily as a prisoner, I am capable of having genuine female friendships.

There are boundaries in place with your male friendships as well, boundaries that must be respected. In our fight for freedom never ask a friend to place themselves into any position that may jeopardize their own freedom. The temptation to capitalize is overwhelming, almost as strong as the sexual impulse. I've seen a person lose sight of the bigger picture and fall into small-mindedness by asking his pastor (who visited weekly) to bring him some contraband. The pastor never came to visit him again.

Respect boundaries. Simple as that. Understand who and what you're dealing with at all times. A "rehabilitated prisoner" is someone who will not be a predator when the opportunity comes his way.

I mention all of this because I know you get it - I'm in the same shoes as you. Real eyes Realize. But at the exact same time we're in a system that intends to end us, to eliminate our genes from the face of the planet. We must sacrifice any/all momentary pleasures in order to achieve security. A real sacrifice will hurt. They're never easy but always required. Integrity requires self-discipline; networking requires integrity. Social change requires networking and a struggle.

"If there is no struggle there is no progress. Those who profess to favor freedom and yet depreciate agitation, are men who want crops without plowing up the ground, they want rain without thunder and lightning. They want the ocean without the awful roar of its many waters. This struggle may be a moral one, or it may be a physical one, and it may be both moral and physical; but it must be a struggle. <u>Power cedes nothing without a demand.</u> It never did and it never will." - Frederick Douglas

People are willing to struggle alongside others who are willing to struggle but nobody is willing to struggle for those who always take the easy way. To move forward, there is no easy way. Victory doesn't come to those who take the easy way. Like Nipsey said, this shit is a marathon.

"The Marathon is all about the work before the celebration, the test of endurance that separates the winners from the rest." – Nipsey

There are many ways to reach out and meet new people. In a later chapter I'll explain several different methods to meet pen pals and build network teams.

The final step to become an agent of social change is to <u>Enlighten</u> others. Many people don't know what's actually going on. Inmates and civilians don't consciously recognize that we have became America's new caste system. Once you've educated yourself it becomes your duty to enlighten others. Sharing knowledge is the debt you owe to knowledge itself. It desires to be shared and applied. After reading a good book, recommend it to another. Speak to others about the power of education and preach how it is our only salvation. Expose the evils of television and despise useless chit chat. Every body has a candle that can be lit.

"Education is not the filling of a bucket. It is the lighting of a fire." - W.B. Yeats.

Spark somebody's flame and inspire them to pass the torch. As light helps us navigate through the dark, education helps us navigate through life. So many people around us are asleep, pushing through life with little more thought than a zombie, doing nothing more than is necessary to sustain a droned existence. Enlighten these people. Be passionate about what you are doing as it is the best emotion that inspires and attracts others. People sense authenticity when someone is passionate about a subject. Use your passion as a means to enlighten people, cause this information to spread like a wild fire - never let it be contained. It's on us as a people to burn down the trees of the system and plant a fresh crop but we can't do it ourselves as individuals.

As an agent of change, you must:

1) Alter the way you see your time

2) Create a routine that pushes you towards your goals AND STICK TO

IT!

3) Educate yourself

4) Network, and respect boundaries

5) Enlighten

Maintain this way of life and you will experience exponential growth within your world and the world of others. Change is coming.

I'll end this chapter with a list of advice (gems) that I took from the autobiography of Albert Woodfox, "Solitary"

1) Move with poise and purpose

2) Be focused on self-education and self-discipline

3) Educate. Agitate. Resist, Be strong. Stay Strong.

4) Do not steal.

5) Arm yourself with knowledge.

6) Go beyond yourself and the influencing of the street, create a different human being

7) Teach yourself the law and file lawsuits against the state.

8) Look outward, beyond prison

9) Stay focused on what's going on in society, not the bullshit that happens inside prison

10) Look for the humanity in each individual

11) Every day you start over

12) Develop a mental toughness

13) Do not allow prison to shape you. Define yourself.

14) Be dedicated to building things, not tearing down

Invictus (Unconquerable)

Out of the night that covers me,

Black as the pit from pole to pole,

I thank whatever gods may be

For my unconquerable soul.

In the fell clutch of circumstance

I have not winced nor cried aloud.

Under the bludgeoning's of chance

My head is bloody, but unbowed.

Beyond this place of wrath and tears

Looms but the Horror of the shade,

And yet the menace of the years

Finds and shall find me unafraid.

It matters not how strait the gate,

How charged with punishments the scroll,

I am the master of my fate,

I am the captain of my soul.

-William Ernest Henley-1875

The Hole

After recently being placed in the hole for being caught with a cell phone, I ran across a friend of mine who had been down there for 7 years. Reflecting on how much had happened in the last 7 years within my life, I felt as if many lifetimes had passed since I'd seen him last. And that entire time, he had been stuck down here in this box. No access to the library, no contact visits, no human contact. No coffee, no adequate food items on commissary. No music, no world. Nothing but a cell and a television, surrounded by a bunch of other voices who sound like they've lost their minds. Just empty ramblings and screaming by this point. To speak with one another, one must yell out the crack of a secured steel door and hope the other can hear you. Or you can talk on the "mini yard" (the recreation area in the hole) for one-hour per day, but you can't see each other or have any physical contact. A brick wall separates you, but you can still speak.

This is where I spoke to my friend, outside where no one else could hear us, and I asked him what does he do to cope with this shit, with solitary confinement, to maintain his sense of being. He told me that after all these years the only way he'd made it through was by cannibalizing parts of his Self. He ate away at any thing positive that arose inside his mind — joy, optimism, happiness, love, empathy - they were the first emotions to go as he fought to sustain his character. After all the positive emotions were gone, he began to eat away at the negative until there was nothing left inside him but bitterness - because that emotion was too bitter to eat. Now there is nothing there but a mind in a shell, trapped in a cage, thinking and thinking and thinking ...

I'll never forget that conversation I had with my friend. It touched me because I've known him for over a decade and it related to what I was going through mentally and emotionally. It taught me to find a better way to cope with solitary. I believed it would be simple enough for me because I was under the impression I'd be out of the hole in less than 30 days. I thought I was just making a quick pit stop and then would be out of there, back to it... but I was wrong. A year later I was released from the hole, and yes I had began to eat away at my emotions. But, learning the lesson from my friend, I chose to eat negative emotions first and to protect my empathy at all costs (easier said than done). The hole affected me - as it always does - but I made it.

Alfred Woodfox's book "Solitary" really hit home when he said:

"There is a part of me that is gone, that has been taken – my soul. I had to sacrifice that part in order to survive. It was the price of being able to make it with my principles intact."

I felt these words to be a different way of expressing the same struggle my friend and I had spoken about. My friend was losing his emotions, Woodfox lost his soul- but my friend is only 7 years in (at the time of this writing) compared to Woodfox's 40 plus. Will my friend lose his soul if not released from solitary confinement? Has he already? And several others besides him have been down there with him for just as long.

In 2018, the United Nations made a statement speaking against the use of solitary confinement:

" "A United Nations expert on torture today called on all countries to ban solitary confinement of prisoners except in very exceptional circumstances and for as short a time as possible.....

Segregation, isolation, separation, cellular, lockdown, Supermax, the hole, Secure Housing Unit (SHU)... whatever the name, solitary confinement should be banned by States as a punishment or extortion technique," UN Special Rapporteur on torture Juan E. Mendez told the General Assembly's third committee, which deals with social, humanitarian and cultural affairs, saying the practice could amount to torture.

"Solitary confinement is a harsh measure which is contrary to rehabilitation, the aim of the penitentiary system," he stressed in presenting his first interim report on the practice, calling it global in nature and subject to widespread abuse.

"Indefinite and prolonged solitary confinement in excess of 15 days should also be subject to an absolute prohibition", he added, citing scientific studies that have established that some lasting mental damage is caused after a few days of social isolation. "

The hole? Extortion techniques? Torture? Contrary to rehabilitation? In excess of 15 days? Lasting mental damage? This is from the United Nations! The leaders of the world! Come on now, what's really going on here?

Research shows that 15 days in solitary confinement can create anxiety, withdrawal, irritability, hallucinations, aggression, paranoia, rage, loss of control, a sense of impending emotional breakdown, hypersensitivity, self-mutilation, and thoughts of suicide.

Many states (including my own) have got around this declaration by redefining the term "solitary confinement" in their statutes, explaining what solitary confinement means to them, how they are morally against it and would never use it. For example, Nebraska says solitary confinement is only when you're placed in a room with no window and can't hear other people.

When I go to the hole (what Nebraska calls Segregated Management) I can hear other people's voices in the hallway and, yes, I have small window that I can look out of to stare at nothing and, yes, eventually I will receive my television. But besides that, I am locked in a cell for 23-hours a day. I am <u>always</u> by myself and I <u>never</u> have any human physical contact. Not even eye contact. One of the most awkward, uncomfortable, anxiety – causing moments for me after being released from the hole is any form of eye contact. Another is being in close proximity of any person, which takes several months to overcome. (I remember instinctively sitting up out of my sleep every time my cellie moved or needed to pee - and he was my homie!) My legs deteriorate from not using them regularly, even if I've exercised the entire stint. They're not accustomed to walking, so a few laps would leave them sore. The lack of sunlight leaves me looking like a vampire. And these are only physical by-products of the hole. The concerning factor is the psychological effects that have occurred, the damage to the mind and emotions that nobody else can see.

The administrations claim we are fine "because they have their TV". Guards say we've "got it made" and that they wish they could lay around and watch TV all day. Oh, do ya? The lack of empathy from these remarks is astounding. I'd rather have them not say anything at all but I understand them to be trying to say "it could be worse"… and they're right. Life could always be worse, for anybody, but that's besides the point. The hole is psychologically damaging and they don't see it.

"If you can't get out of the cell nothing they give you makes a difference. The pressure of being in the cell never goes away. The fight for sanity never goes away. You want me to believe I'm OK when I'm not OK, I can't give you specifics on how being in solitary has affected me but I can tell you without a doubt it has affected me". - Albert Woodfox

Without a doubt, it has affected me - as it has affected millions of others as well who have suffered solitary confinement.

They've come up with all sorts of language loopholes to get around the fact that solitary confinement is still in widespread use amongst America- for punishment. It's now illegal to sanction somebody to solitary confinement as a form of punishment, but if I am placed in solitary confinement after misbehaving, how is this not punishment?

In a general population setting (in Nebraska) we're allowed over 6 hours "out-of-cell" time per day. We're allowed to receive contact-visits every week and can use the telephone up to two-hours every day. Tablets are given to us that we use for listening to music and to email our family/friends day and night. We're also allowed to purchase "personal property" such as clothes, shoes, TV, lamp, beard trimmers, watch, thermals, etc.

Upon violating a rule (such as getting caught with a cell phone), your hands are cuffed behind your back and shackles placed around ankles as you're being escorted to an entirely different section of the prison called the Segregated Management Unit (SMU). You are given an orange jumpsuit to wear (replacing the regular Khakis) and you are locked into a cold cell with nothing in it, by yourself. You have a thin mattress and a blanket, pen and paper.. that's it. After your cell is closed and secure, then and only then, do the guards remove your handcuffs through a hatch in the door... the same hatch used to deliver food and anything else to us. But that door will not be opened again.

Everything has been stripped from you. You will not be able to make a phone call in those first 48 hours - not even to notify your family that you've been taken to the hole. And when you do finally get a call, you now only get 15-minutes per week, whereas in general pop, you're receiving 2-hours of phone calls per day! You no longer have your tablet used for sending/receiving emails. Any communication with the outside world is deadened immediately.

You will receive one-hour out of your cell, 5 days a week, spent at a "mini yard" that is no bigger than your cell- and you're alone. That is your recreation time.

You will receive NO in-person contact-visits for any reason. No skype visits via Zoom. If your family/friends would like to see you, they must drive all the way to the prison (an hour away from any city) to visit you for one-hour through a computer screen! Naturally, people stop coming to visit under those conditions.

It's simply you inside of a cage-like an animal-with a bunch of screaming voices that surround you (day and night) because everyone else is by themselves, locked in a cage too. But you can't see their faces from your window... you can only hear their screams. But no, you're not being punished for your behavior...

"Of course not, we would never do this to punish you. We've determined that your presence in general population creates a risk to yourself and others, so that is why we did this to you. We're not punishing you, silly - we're reclassifying you to Long Term Restrictive Housing status. No no no, see, we'll punish you by taking your commissary and phone privileges for a month, but the hole isn't used to punish you. Now sit there and think about your behavior!" says the administration (with a smile) as we ask how/why they still utilize the hole to punish us.

The American Heritage dictionary defines the word punishment as: 1. The imposition of a penalty for wrong doing. 2. A penalty for wrong doing. 3. Rough treatment or use.

The loophole discovered by prison administrators is that as long as they don't write down on paper "said prisoner is receiving segregation as a penalty for his misconduct " then they're legally protected. But that doesn't mean they're not doing it! They still use segregation as a punishment, they just don't verbalize that they're using it as a punishment.

One more time, let us review the changes one must face upon being placed in segregation:

1) 6-hours out-of-cell-time <u>per day</u> TO 5-hours out-of-cell <u>per week</u>;

2) In-person contact-visits every week TO no contact-visits;

3) Access to library books TO no access to library books;

4) Access to personal clothes/shoes TO orange jumpsuits/flip flops;

5) Send/Receive emails freely TO no emails at all;

6) Two-hours of phone calls per day TO 15-minutes of calls per week

.

But no, this is not "rough treatment" according to the admin. This is not any form of punishment for your behavior. This is not solitary confinement. This is not counter productive to rehabilitation. Your family/friends won't suffer due to these changes and your relationships will remain healthy as ever.

And they say, "well, maybe you should have thought about this before you did what you did" - which only proves segregation to be a punishment.

This is all bullshit. Hogwash. And everyone is aware of it. There's nothing "rehabilitative" about it. Segregation is detrimental to society in every way.

Honestly, I believe that it should be legal to punish us with segregation but illegal to use segregation as a classification housing unit. The reason I give for this is because the classification process (Long Term Restrictive Housing) is used to house us in segregation for extensively long periods of time (13 months for possession of a cell phone) and indefinitely in other cases (like my friend previously mentioned). If segregation was only allowed to be used for punishment (not classification) they could tell us "You've been sentenced to 6 months in segregated management" - which means we would know that we're getting out of the hole in 6 months (as long a we don't misbehave).

As a classification we have no idea when we'll be released from the hole, if ever. Each individual is reviewed every 90-days on a case-by-case basis. You have no idea when you're leaving segregation. Like I said... I had believed I'd be down there no longer than 30-days but I was stuck for 13 months.

This form of punishment (the classification process) is the worst form of segregative punishment - and it's legal. They're allowed to do it. None of it makes any sense. How is it torture for the administration to "punish" you with 15 days in segregation, but rehabilitative to classify you to LTRH and keep you 5 years in segregation? The entire concept is morally wrong, inhumane, and needs to be eliminated from the penitentiary system.

The administration will argue that there is a real danger to letting some of these guys intermingle with the general population. Okay, in some cases... maybe there is. But what does this have to do with the "changes" imposed on people's way of living placed in the segregation management unit? If SMU is to keep people "segregated" from general population (and is not used to punish) why can't they just be moved to the cell by themselves, with controlled movement, but still have two-hours of phone calls every day? - still have emails? - still have all of their personal property and access to books from the library? - still have the option to buy coffee and other food items? - still have contact visits with family/friends?

In reality, they could still allow all of these things to people housed in SMU. But, in reality, SMU is used to punish. Simple and plain, there's no way around it. And this abuse of power needs to be recognized. Things must be changed. If not, sooner or later, all of our souls will be stolen from us.

"I had never had my own emotions be so completely out of my control, and clearly hurting myself or making myself vulnerable to power-tripping guards didn't serve me, but was it up to me how I reacted? Did "free will" exist in a context where I was so highly triggered and

frightened, or had my reactions become automatic? Without freedom, was there still an "I'? And if so, who was "I' responsible to? I'd close my eyes and imagine myself back in my solitary cell. What were the sounds? I'd hear footsteps coming down the prison corridor, the constant static of air coming down through the vent, a faucet running in someone else's cell. I'd feel my body clench, slightly, my face harden and my heart beat a little faster. "

-Sarah Shourd, served 410 days solitary confinement in Iranian prison

Don't Let a Failure Stop You

Two men looked from prison bars,

One saw mud, the other stars.

Your attitude towards life determines what your life will become. Yes, we fucked up and ended up in a bad situation. A prison cell is only relatable if you've experienced it personally, which tends to alienate us from others in society. They don't understand the damage caused to us psychologically...But we don't understand their struggles, damages, or traumas either. Each of our lives are completely different. We've all made mistakes within life, some mistakes more severe than others, but thing about it is... most people feel like failures inside. And this is an attitude.

There's a difference between never being satisfied and feeling like a failure. No matter how many times we've been told that failure is bound to happen, over and over again, it still doesn't let us feel any better about it because let's face it... failing sucks. But it doesn't have to be the death of us or the end of accomplishing our dreams and goals, our career. We can still have goals, even after having failed. The classic example is the story of Thomas Edison, who failed 1,000 times before he ever got his light bulb to work. Imagine your experiments failing over and over and over and over again...1,000 times... and how exhausted you would feel. But it's the attitude with how we view our failures that either exhausts or motivates us. In the case of Edison, he had a dream of inventing the light bulb - and he believed it was possible. He knew it was possible, he just didn't know how to make it happen. But he got started, and with every failure he learned a valuable lesson - he learned what didn't work!

Viewing a failure as a lesson - learning what doesn't work- turns things into a matter of elimination. You believe your dreams are possible, you know they are possible, you're just not certain about how you're going to manifest them. Your first idea is rarely your best idea, but you have to fail from it in order to learn that it wasn't the best idea. Once you know something is possible, like success, the only difference between you and the next man becomes who is more determined to achieve what they both know is possible. Edison could have easily told himself "I know it's possible to make a light bulb but that's too much work for me. I'll leave that task to the next man" and Edison could have been just like the majority of people.

But he was determined to succeed... and he knew that he would succeed long as he never gave up. He was determined to see it through, and became the archetype of persistence. 1,000 failures before succeeding in his dream which revolutionized the entire world! I'm sitting here right now at 6:00 AM able to write these words while my cellmate sleeps thanks to Edison and his 1,000 failures. My lamp shines just enough light to let me do my work without disrupting my cellie's sleep - and I thank Edison for his invention. He lit up the world! I idolize his determination and persistence, as should you. After all, determination and persistence are the secrets to thinking and growing rich. That's a perfect example of how it is not knowledge which equals power - but applied knowledge. We all know that determination and persistence inevitably lead us to success, but most of us don't apply this knowledge within their lives.

We're going to fail. That's just the fact of the matter. Being resilient allows you to fail without losing hope, without giving up, which is why resiliency is one of my virtues of integrity. Being resilient allows you to bounce back, to get up after you've fallen, and see how to try it differently next time. It's imperative because, time and time again, every success story begins with a long list of failures.

Mike Enemigo is the owner of The Cell Block Publishing, and is also serving a natural life sentence. He lost somewhere between $10-20,000 before ever reaching any level of success. He failed several times but continued forward, and now his books are read by prisoners all across the country. Had he given up and quit, I'd have never read his book called "Jailhouse Publishing" which inspired me to get on my shit and make my dreams happen. This book you're reading now may have never ended up in your hands had Mike Enemigo quit trying to achieve his dreams after having lost his first 5 bands. That's a lot of money to most prisoners-and most people. I heard on CNN the other day that most Americans don't have $400 put away in a rainy-day fund for them to fall back on in case of an emergency (sad, but probably true). This being so, imagine how a prisoner would feel after losing thousands of dollars trying to make a dream come true when he has no way to make that money back. Quick shout out to Mike Enemigo - you good at what you do.

We can't be scared to fail. And we can't be too attached to our money. We gotta be able to risk it for the biscuit - which I mean to say invest our money into our dreams and goals - even if we lose it all. Drake said *"You lose some, you win some. Long as the outcome is income"*. It takes losses to make a profit... Jeff Bezos knows that. You WILL FAIL-but see it as part of your education, your experiences in life that you learn from.

Experience has always been the best teacher. How many times did you fall off your bike before you learned how to ride it? These are lessons we learned as children but have forgotten as adults, realizing it's the same principle. The fear we have of failing stops people from even trying. It creates inaction. The basketball player misses 100% of the shots he doesn't take. We see it every time we call home with a brilliant business idea to get rich and change our lives forever... the first thing we hear is "That won't work" and then they change the subject to a lighter topic. You're thinking "Damn... I just explained to you exactly how and why it will work, how and why there is a demand for this service, and without any consideration you say that won't work." Got me in here feeling like Edison - I know it will work, I just need to figure out the best way to get it done through trial and error.

It's not necessarily that people don't believe in you or your ideas, it's that their own personal fear of failure has bred inactivity. They'd rather convince themselves that they're perfectly fine at the bottom of the class system, working 40-hours a week for a measly check, than to face the possibility of trying and failing.

This form of complacency is sinful to those who are ambitious, determined to achieve their dreams. The correct response to a good idea is "That will work... we just need to figure out how, and fail until we succeed."

A "burning the boat" mentality is required in order to overcome complacency, doubt, laziness, and fear of failure. "Burning the boats" was what generals did upon arriving at new territory that they had planned to conquer through war. Soldiers would be nervous due to the size of the opposing army, which would take away from their focus on the fight as they contemplated how and when to retreat back to their boats, back safety. To eliminate any backwards thinking or thoughts of retreat, generals would burn the boats so that there was nothing but the sea behind them. Either win or die, no other options. This would fill soldiers with a new urge to overcome the enemy, bringing unbelievable levels of success. But if you always have a boat to run back to when things get scary, you'll never give your all.

Success requires your all. Victory requires burning the boats. Set your mind on something and allow nothing to deter you from achieving this goal. It's do or die... no shades of gray between the black and white when it comes to whether or not you achieve your goals. You did or you didn't.

Failures are only tests that the goddess of success puts everyone through to judge who is worthy. Everything isn't for everybody. Overcoming your failures and continuing towards your goals is persistence - a virtue required by the goddess of success. You are worthy. You just gotta find it within yourself and bring it to the surface. It's the attitude with which you view life and the failures within it. Change your attitude and don't let it get you down. Be resilient.

<u>10 ways to build Resilience</u> (provided by American Psychology Association)

1) Make connections with others

2) Avoid seeing crises as insurmountable problems

3) Accept that change is part of life

4) Move toward your goals

5) Take decisive actions

6) Look for opportunities for self-discovery

7) Nurture a positive view of yourself

8) Keep things in perspective

9) Maintain a hopeful outlook

10) Take care of yourself

Highly resilient people are flexible, they adapt to new circumstances quickly, they thrive in constant change, they expect to bounce back, and they have an ability to create good luck out of what others see as bad luck.

"I don't put much stock in the idea of luck. I think that things go well or not so well for people based on their actions. I believe that for the most part you create your own luck by working hard, practicing self-discipline, remaining persistent and making personal growth a daily priority. Add that to the blessings of a loving God, and you don't need to think about luck." -John C. Maxwell

It's not a matter of luck, or God dropping success into your lap. It's about who can overcome failure, who can be honest with themselves. about their strengths and weaknesses, who can maintain a positive attitude, and who is willing to burn their boats. Success is a lifestyle, it's a mind-state. It's not winning the lottery or achieving overnight success. Mark Cuban, a billionaire, said it took him 10 years to become an overnight success. People don't see all the hardwork it takes to finally make it. And once you do, it appears like you came out of nowhere and got rich overnight. Successful people know this isn't true. They've just learned how to "fail forward".

15 Steps to Failing Forward

1) Realize there is a major difference between average people and achieving people.

2) Learn a new definition of failure.

3) Remove the "you" from failure.

4) Take action and reduce your fear.

5) Change your response to failure by accepting responsibility.

6) Don't let the failure from outside get inside you.

7) Say goodbye to yesterday.

8) Change yourself, and your world changes.

9) Get over yourself and start giving yourself.

10) Find the benefit in every bad situation.

11) If at first you do succeed, try something harder.

12) Learn from a bad experience and make it a good experience.

13) Work on the weakness that weakens you.

14) Understand there's not much difference between failure and success.

15) Get up, get over it, get going.

Learn more about each of these steps from John C. Maxwell's book "Failing Forward". This book is great for anyone struggling to overcome their negative attitude about failing. John C. Maxwell turns the word "forward" into an acronym:

Finalize your goal.

Order your plans.

Risk failing by taking action.

Welcome mistakes.

Advance based on your character.

Reevaluate your progress continually.

Develop new strategies to succeed.

"Every time you face mistakes and attempt to move forward in spite of them is a test of character. There always comes a time when giving up is easier than standing up, when giving in looks more attractive than digging in. And in these moments, character may be the only thing you have to draw on to keep you going." - John C. Maxwell

Once you've overcome the fear of failure, what is left to get in your way? Once you realize that your fear of failure is something that comes out of yourself, you see that you have been the only thing in your way. Why continue to allow yourself to stop yourself from achieving success? It's not an easy task, not at all.

Benjamin Franklin said *"There are three things extremely hard: steel, a diamond, and to know one's self."* The first victory must be over the self, over your attitude, and then everything else will fall into place. We can't allow the fact that we're incarcerated to be an excuse to not make something of ourselves. To not make use of our time, no matter how long or short it may be, is still an excuse – and excuses never lead to achievement. If we let these people take away our determination, to destroy our will, then and only then, have they defeated us.

Remember: ***They tried to bury us... they didn't know we were seeds.***

Long as we continue to push forward, the battle rages. And my goal is to win our freedom. To maintain our freedom. And I believe in this goal, I know it can happen. Therefore, I'm willing to fail 1,000 times in order to achieve this goal. They've got us down bad right now, I can't argue with that. But no matter how bad it gets, it's not over until we let it be over- until we stop fighting for what we want. I've seen it take people 17 years of fighting their appeal before finally receiving the decision from a judge to overturn a conviction and let someone go home. Had he lost hope or belief at any time throughout them 17 years and gave up working on his appeal, he'd have never went home. Sometimes I've seen it take even longer than that. Laws can change that bring hope to a situation that once seemed hopeless - but the trick is to never lose hope in the first place.

When a law does change, your chances of going home depend on your behavior of the prior decade when all felt hopeless. Those who gave up and gave in to the bullshit of prison life may not be released at the time when the new law is passed, whereas the prisoner who showed a record of rehabilitation while all felt hopeless may receive an immediate release. The difference between the two is the attitude each maintained throughout life's failures and hardships. Growing doesn't make you "fake", and being "real" doesn't mean acting stupid. *Real eyes Realize.*

You are not weak....weak people don't survive in here. You've got the same ability to do what any other successful person has done. You just do it. Put one foot in front of the other and go. Life is a marathon; it's not about who can run the fastest, but who can run the longest. We can't sprint to success. It's one foot after the other, again and again, don't quit even when it burns, even when you're tired, even when you're out of breath... you keep going.

"He who every morning plans the transactions of the day and follows out that plan carries a thread that will guide him through the labyrinth of the most busy life... But where no plan is laid, where the disposal of time is surrendered merely to the chance of incident, chaos will soon reign." - Victor Hugo

We must not let chaos reign.

I will end this chapter leaving you with Napolean Hill's "Thirty Major Causes of Failure and his Symptoms of Lack of Persistence" found within his classic book, *"Think And Grow Rich"*.

<u>Thirty Major Causes of Failure</u>

1) Unfavorable hereditary background (unfixable)

2) Lack of a well-defined purpose in life

3) Lack of ambition to aim above mediocrity

4) Insufficient education

5) Lack of Self-Discipline

6) Ill Health

7) Unfavorable environmental influences during childhood

8) Procrastination

9) Lack of Persistence

10) Negative Personality

11) Lack of controlled sexual urge

12) Uncontrolled desire of "Something for Nothing"

13) Lack of a well-defined Power of Decision

14) One or more of the Six Basic Fears

15) Wrong selection of mate in marriage

16) Over- Caution

17) Wrong selection of business associates

18) Superstition and Prejudice

19) Wrong selection of Vocation

20) Lack of concentration of effort

21) The habit of indiscriminate spending

22) Lack of Enthusiasm

23) Intolerance

24) Intemperance

25) Inability to cooperate with others

26) Possession of Power NOT acquired through self-effort

27) Intentional Dishonesty

28) Egotism and Vanity

29) Guessing instead of Thinking

30) Lack of Capital

<u>Symptoms of Lack of Persistence</u>

1) Failure to recognize and to clearly define exactly what one wants

2) Procrastination, with or without cause

3) Lack of interest in acquiring specialized knowledge

4) Indecision, NOT facing issues squarely

5) The habit of Relying upon Alibis instead of creating definite plans for

   the solution of problems

6) Self-Satisfaction

7) Indifference (too ready to compromise)

8) The habit of Blaming Others for one's mistakes, and accepting unfavorable circumstances as being unavoidable

9) Weakness of Desire

10) Willingness, even Eagerness, to quit at first sign of defeat

11) Lack of Organized Plans, placed in writing where they may be analyzed

12) The habit of neglecting to move on ideas, or to grasp opportunity when it presents itself

13) WISHING instead of WILLING

14) The habit of compromising with POVERTY instead of aiming at riches. General absence of Ambition to be, to do, and to own.

15) Searching for all the short-cuts to riches, trying to GET without GIVING a fair equivalent.

16) FEAR OF CRITICISM! failure to create plans and put them into action, because of what other people will think, do, or say.

Appearances

Not all of us are supermodels, or have been blessed with naturally good looks (subjective), but never use this as an excuse to neglect your appearance. Taking care of yourself symbolizes respect for yourself. If you respect yourself, others will respect you. People can only respect you as much as you respect yourself... So what does it reflect to others when you come out of your cell "dusted and disgusted", or hair all over the place, or face unshaven and wild, clothes not ironed, breath stinkin' and face not washed?

It should be a sin to even speak in the morning before you brush your teeth and wash your face. Get out of the bunk and get yourself together. Make your bed in the morning and take care of yourself. Look in the mirror and give yourself a positive affirmation.

Radiating positivity and cleanliness attracts positivity and cleanliness. Reflect what you are in search of. Two people may have the exact same character traits, but more respect will be given to the one who maintains his appearance and doesn't carry himself like a bum.

An ugly person (subjective) can appear attractive - or more attractive - by taking care of himself, maintaining proper hygiene, exercising, and respecting himself.

Aesthetics are important, little tweaks to one's appearance that catch the eyes of another. Simple aesthetic items would include any jewelry, or wearing jeans (instead of khakis) for no special reason – just to remind people you're still a human. Aesthetics can include craft items people create, make-up materials, different designs in one's style of hair clothing preference. Aesthetics are used to catch the eye without screaming "look at me!"

"Good looks" definitely make it easier but being able to catch someone's attention is most important. All in all, "good looks" are in the eye of the beholder, but nobody is attracted to the person who doesn't take care of themselves or has bad hygiene. And these things are a matter of choice: one chooses whether or not they wake up and brush their teeth first thing in the morning, one chooses whether they wash their face and make sure no crusties are in their eyes; one chooses whether they wear wrinkled up clothes; one chooses to take actions each and every morning to develop self-respect and, in effect, respect from others.

Take care of yourself, maintain your appearance. You know what I'm talking about, you don't need to be told how to maintain your appearance but sometimes people need to be reminded as to why it's important. If you know others who neglect their appearance, you'll notice an underlying depression or sadness in their character. Remind them of what needs to be done as a beginning step towards feeling better about themselves and about life.

Organize Your Mind

"Your world is an outer manifestation of your inner thoughts and attitudes. As within, so without." -Greek philosopher, Hermes.

If you fail to plan then plan to fail.

We've all heard it before... but then why do we still fail to plan? Just another case of not applying one's knowledge they've obtained. Or, maybe one knows that they're suppose to plan but really doesn't know how to or where to start. Sometimes it can be difficult to plan but it's something that we have to start doing.

99% of prisoners I've met wake in the morning (or afternoon) with no idea about what they're going to do for the day. In order to not even think about it, the first thing they do upon opening their eyes is turn the TV on, numb the mind and all thought processes. Not only do they not know what their plan is for the day, they probably didn't wake up at a set, predetermined time- they slept until their body wouldn't let them any more because they didn't want to face the day. This attitude (chaos) isn't going to work if your goal is to achieve any meaningful type of success. One must bring order out of this chaos; you must organize your mind.

Your daily routine (discussed earlier) is the initial step in one's organizing of the mind. If you want to plan but don't know how, begin with your daily routine. You can't plan years into the future if you can't plan your daily activities. Conquer the small things first. Many businesses fail within the first few years simply because they failed to plan ahead of time. Chaos must not be allowed to reign supreme.

Question: Do you want to be rich? Assuming you answered yes, you must learn to do what the rich people do. It's not a coincidence that rich people have similar habits and routines. It's principle that allows one to become rich and it's as simple as following the principles. Rich people keep cool in tense situations, maintaining control over their emotions. They maintain a "To-do" list. They don't watch too much TV (one hour a day).

They read educational books to broaden their financial IQ. They network with other people of integrity. They follow a healthy diet. They listen to podcasts or audio books instead of negative music. They avoid gambling and vices. They invest. They get up early to get their day started. They look forward to the days, weeks, months, years, decades ahead of them. They don't look backwards, they don't moonwalk into the future. They face daily challenges and problems.

If you don't know any rich people, read about some rich people and learn from their daily habits. I guarantee you none of them wake up to a blunt every morning. Facts. Rich people don't just do things without a legitimate reason. There is a legitimate reason for every habit they've acquired, because these habits push them toward their goals.

A lot of people despise the rich, telling themselves "If I had the same opportunities or privileges they had in life, I'd be rich too." Maybe true, maybe not, but this attitude is one of resentment and envy. It's a justification to not get it yourself. You've heard about those rich people who appear to have wonderful lives but still aren't happy - that's because being rich is all they've known! They've never struggled, never been at the bottom. They've never survived poverty. And, because of this, they have no other experiences to compare their life to. They can't be happy because a struggle is part of our nature, a part of life. Without it, the riches mean nothing to a person.

Someone who's been through the most finally comes up on a legit bag and starts touching some real money - it's going to be so much easier for that person to find peace and happiness because they should always remember what life was like without it. They have reason to be grateful. Don't envy or resent people. Focus on your own journey and realize how different it will be for you once you achieve your goals. If anything, aim to make those same unhappy rich people envious and resentful of you because they see how happy you are with your life. The pursuit of happiness... the journey and the goal. Money won't make you happy, but it'll make you happier... that's for sure.

Rather than envy other people, we should celebrate human accomplishment. If they can do it, you can do it... and somebody else's accomplishment should give you hope for the future. Envy and jealousy are poisonous emotions. We don't entertain that. Real eyes Realize. Transmute those negative emotions into positive ones, poverty into riches.

To get there, we must be organized and in control of our every action. Especially our bad spending habits. I'm constantly surprised by how many people live a life of "spending more than they earn". The math is simple, spending more than you earn equals DEBT. Debt does not bring us closer to our goals and dreams. I'm not referring to debt acquired from loans that you invest into business activities which, in theory, should pay themselves off and bring you profits. I'm talking about the use of credit as a way of living throughout each day, and then every dollar you ever earn goes to paying down debt, and then you get in more debt because you just paid all your money to getting out of old debt. It makes no sense to live like this. It isn't natural. That's some American shit right there, one of the problems we have as country. <u>We consume more than we produce</u>. And that's a negative mathematically. It can never work, it can never last. To get ahead, you must change your bad spending habits. Easier said than done.

First thing you need to do is devise a Balance Sheet. A Balance Sheet will help you bring order to your chaos and show you on paper how you need to adapt yourself to a more natural way of living. Be in harmony with your own personal nature; flow with it, not against it. Indulgence is a sacrament; over-indulgence is stupidity. Find your balance.

Making a Balance Sheet is easy enough. If you understand how to add/subtract numbers, you've got what it takes. Use a calculator if it makes things easier. Draw a box like this:

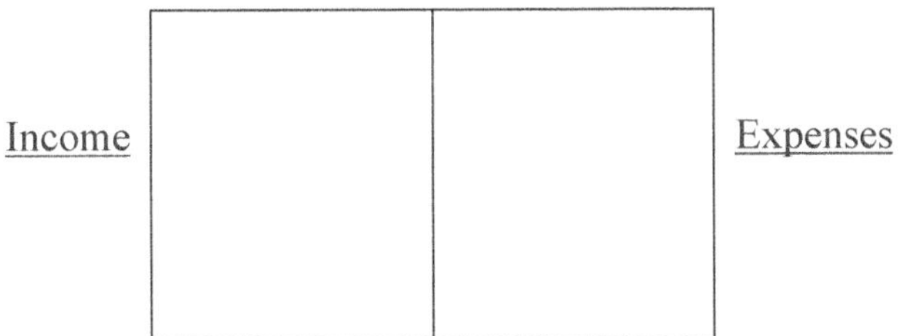

This box is used to separate your "Income" (how much money you make each month) from your "Expenses" (your bills, how much money you must pay each month). If we were to use our typical worker from society, their Balance Sheet may look like this:

Monthly

Income	Job's Paycheck - $2,500 Donate plasma- $320 Babysitting - $300	Rent - $1,000 Cell phone - $100 Food-$300 Gas-$100 Cigarettes - $100 Savings- $500	Expenses

Once they've separated the two categories, documenting everything they are 100% sure will result in Income/Expense (don't include any "hopes and dreams" in your income AND include all vices within expenses) then you add up the total from each category.

Income	Expenses
2,500	1,000
320	100
300	300
$3,120	100
	100
	500
	$2,100

Now you subtract the expenses from the income (Income minus Expense)

$$3,120 \text{ (Income)}$$
$$-2,100 \text{ (Expense)}$$
$$\$1,020$$

This total ($1,020) is the pocket change money left over for the month. The example of our citizen must adapt to a lifestyle of spending no more than $1,020 per month on pleasures and extracurricular activities. Going out to the bar or to the movies, buying new clothes, eating out at restaurants, etc... all of this must never go beyond the amount of money that is left after expenses are paid for the month.

To organize this routine even more and concentrate one's available spending, this citizen would divide 1,020 by 4 (weeks in the month) to determine how much money is available to spend each week ($255 week, in this example). Long as this individual doesn't spend any more than $255 per week, they are living within their means. Spending more than $255 per week (through use of credit cards and borrowing) one is consuming more than they produce. One way of living carries you forward in life, one brings you backwards.

Let's use examples of a few different prisoners I've met within my time. We won't use any names in true spirit of a convict.

Prisoner #1

He's been blessed to have parents (divorced) who each have agreed to send him $50 per month. He also has a girlfriend who was sending him $100 per month, and he receives $25 per month from the prison for his unit job. The income side of his Balance Sheet looks like this:

Income		Expenses
	Dad-$50	
	Mom-$50	
	Girl-$100	
	Pay-$25	

Prisoner #1 had an income of $225 per month. Not bad for your typical prisoner. But, this guy had a few expenses he dealt with on a monthly basis as well, which came in the form of vices. He gambled approximately $10/week on parley tickets ($40/month), he gambled approximately $20/week at the poker table ($80/month), plus, he'd picked up a smoking habit (K2) which is the itch that can't get scratched. He spent

typically around $200/month (at least) on his K2 habit. Then, every time

he got high, he'd get hungry but because he spends all his money on vices,

he never has any food in his room. Therefore, he borrows food from "the

store man" who charges interest. Borrowing food runs him about

$50/month.

Here is what Prisoner #1's completed Balance Sheet looks like:

Monthly

Income	Dad-$50	Parley-$40	Expenses
	Mom-$50	Poker-$80	
	Girl-$100	K2- $200	
	Pay-$25	Food-$50	
	Income = 225	Expenses=310	

Do the math (Income- Expenses) and our guy is in the negative

each month $145. Each month Prisoner #1 runs up $145 in debt that he

really doesn't have the money to pay. Luckily for him, every few months

there's a "drought" where there's no K2 available and the gambling gets

shut down so he has a brief period of paying down his debts (he never gets

completely out of debt) just enough to get even deeper again once the dope

hits. At one point, pressure started coming down on him to get his debts paid, which caused him to start putting pressure on his girlfriend and family for more money each month. The stress and arguments caused his girlfriend to leave him, and his family (now aware of his addictions) began to only send money to his personal account (no longer doing cashapp transactions for him). This only made matters worse for him, making it harder to pay his debts - and he still has his vices. This goes nowhere good. Prisoner #1 resorts to brewing "hooch" (homemade alcohol) and holding people's contraband to pay off his debts. He can't keep up this lifestyle and shit gets too heavy for him, so what's he do? He files for bankruptcy. In other words, he checks in to protective custody. Consuming more than he produced collapsed on top of him, as it will do to any individual who believes they can live outside of their means.

Prisoner #2 is another example of a guy I know. He doesn't happen to have any money or income from his parents but he has a wife who does what she can for him. She's able to always send $100 per month, as well as pay for their phone calls. Prisoner #2 also holds a decent job that pays him another $100 per month. Now this guy doesn't have any vices but he loves to exercise and eat well. A healthy diet is important to him, as well as going to bed full every night. To live like this costs him about $50 per week at the commissary. So here is what Prisoner # 2's Balance Sheet looks like:

Monthly

Income	Wife-$100 Job-$100	Food- $200	Expenses

Income = $200   Expenses = $200

Prisoner #2 has adapted to his circumstances and lives exactly within his means. He consumes exactly what he produces and runs into no immediate problems because of it. He's the example of a citizen living paycheck to paycheck- never getting ahead but never falling behind. Simply existing and trying to enjoy the moment.

Now, Prisoner #3 is a different kind of guy. He doesn't have much but he has an eye for opportunity. Prisoner #3 prides himself and derives joy from "living off the land". Therefore he doesn't ask his girlfriend for anything besides to put money on her phone so he can call and to handle his cashapp transactions for him (because he personally can't). Having worked his way into a job that pays him $100 per month, he has his own money to invest in little hustles he'd discovered. The first pay check that Prisoner #3 received, he put $50 into his savings account and spent $50 on food items, which were the ingredients used to make brownie cakes and candy balls (that sell for double the price of the ingredients). He also bought a "quarter pack" (25) of soda pop tokens that he would lend out to reliable people "2 for 3" back in return. Jotting down the numbers and doing the math, Prisoner #3 would make $100 from the $50 he invested, which he could make happen every week!

Prisoner #3 is a man of discipline who understood that success requires sacrifice. He receives 3 meals per day for free from the kitchen and has no rent to pay each month for shelter, no bills at all. He chose to see this as an opportunity, rather than a hardship, and took advantage of it. To him, there was no need to buy excess items from the commissary - he saw that as giving his hard-earned money back to his oppressors. He grew up in poverty so 3 meals a day was enough for him to survive on. However, he did drink coffee every day long as he could always afford it, which he could. It helped him be productive and focused. He also knew he needed to buy hygiene items and maintain personal appearances. These expenses ran him about $10 per week at the store.

Based upon these numbers, the Balance Sheet looks like this:

Monthly

<table>
<tr><td rowspan="3">Income</td><td>Candy/brownie-</td><td>Ingredients- $200</td><td rowspan="3">Expenses</td></tr>
<tr><td>$400</td><td>Personal care- $40</td></tr>
<tr><td>Paycheck- $100</td><td>Savings- $50</td></tr>
</table>

Income: $500   Expenses: $290

Income minus Expenses (500-290), Prisoner #3 is in the positive each month-without any financial assistance from the outside world. After his first month of positive cash flow, he began placing his entire paycheck into his savings account each month ($100). That's $1,200 per year he would save, as well as pulling in a minimum of $160 a month of profits from his candy/brownie / token business.

Because he believes the universe blesses those who are generous (and partly because he's just a good guy) he always gave away 10% of his profits (about $15) per month of candy or cake to those who didn't have much. It was spiritual to him, giving was important.

Prisoner #3 is an example of a guy who is making the best out of a bad situation and not allowing his past mistakes to stop him from achieving his goals. And his goals were always much bigger than a savings account and $150 a month. These were just the initial steps taken. He knew that this hustle and his sacrifice, his persistence and determination, were required of him in order to achieve his larger goals.

How do you think Prisoner #3 spent his days? Do you think he slept until noon every morning and then spent his time watching TV or playing spades? Do you think he chased a K2 high or gambled away all his money? Of course not. He devised a routine and he stuck to it, day after day, month after month, year after year. He worked a job Monday through Friday from 8am to 4pm, but he woke up at 6AM every morning. Each morning he would wake up, make his bed, brush his teeth and wash his face, stretch out his body, and make a cup of coffee. As he drank his coffee, he'd read financial books for almost an hour until 7AM. After finished with his daily reading, he'd turn on GMA just to catch the news scrolling across the bottom line-he wouldn't even have the volume up. It'd stay on mute. After reading the bottom line, the TV was off again. A quick positive affirmation while staring in the mirror before the day room opened and he was off to work.

Getting off work at 4PM he'd immediately do a 45-minutte high intensity exercise routine, something different each day, and would then take a shower.

By this time would be dinner, which he would eat and then return "home" (his cell) to begin his hobby/hustle - his bakery. Washing up and using latex gloves, he'd spend from 6PM to 7:30PM whipping up his brownie cakes and candy balls. As his brand name had developed and became credible (integrity), people began purchasing orders of his products ahead of time...so at 7:30pm he'd just make his deliveries and then socialize until about 8pm before we were locked down for the night within our cells. Then it was time for his phone call with Baby, which was usually for about an hour.

By 10pm he was in bed going to sleep. Every day went like this, Monday through Friday. The weekends he would take to relax, write letters, and network socially with the people around him in his prison. It was a nice, balanced routine. Prisoner #3 had organized his mind, therefore, his life.

Out of Prisoners 1, 2, or 3 - who do you think was happier within their inner life? Who was more at peace? Confident with their self and optimistic? Lived a more fulfilling existence? - Prisoner #3, and he was the only one who had no financial support from the free world.

An entire book is in the works of being wrote about Prisoner #3, about his life and what has became of it. Like I said, this routine was only the first step taken on the ladder of his larger goal- his dream - and "oh my god" did he manifest it! This separate book exemplifies where he's at now in life and how much he's accomplished, starting from nothing. He's the best example of a guy who never allowed any excuses to hold him back and today he's more successful than many people in the free world - but is still in prison.

What made him different from most people was that he had a vision of what was possible given the means at his disposal. He wasn't unrealistic in his dreams but reached as high as his reality could allow him to reach. Then he organized his mind by devising a step-by-step plan, a blue print or roadmap that he was determined to follow til the end. Many changes were made within his plans as his education and opportunities increased but the "end game" remained the same.. Just like every other successful person, he made mistakes along the way and suffered failures in the form of losses and setbacks. But he was resilient. I learned a lot from this man and am honored to be able to share his story and knowledge with others.

The key is to organize your mind. Look into the future and plan for it. This is what we all must do as prisoners - especially if you have an outdate to look forward to. We must never allow our incarceration to be the excuse that holds us back from success. Live within your means. Even if you don't yet have the discipline to make the sacrifices required of real success, at least choose to live within your means - as did Prisoner #2. This is a way to develop self-discipline and begin to make the sacrifices necessary to get ahead. But never be the guy who consumes more than he can produce. This is counterproductive - to self and to society. Living in debt is what gives an institution (such as a bank or the federal reserve) control over our lives. We desire freedom; debt is opposed to this desire.

To do this you must operate your lifestyle (or your business) as if bad times are always here... that is Jeff Bezos' "Day 1" philosophy. Never get ahead of yourself and always expect the worst.

While living your life or operating your business, always ask yourself:

Am I building a pipeline or hauling buckets?

Am I working harder or am I working smarter?

Hauling buckets is fine, initially, but the goal would be to build a pipeline which would deliver the water without any physical labor. Smarter.

About a decade ago, a fellow inmate of mine gave me a pamphlet of information that he'd acquired over the years. This was close to the beginning of my prison sentence but he'd already been down almost three decades. We're not very close, and I don't even know where he's at anymore, but he's the first person I recognized as being More Than An Inmate. Within this pamphlet of information, I read a paragraph that changed my life because it changed the way I view wealth. I don't know where he gathered this or if it's something he wrote himself, but it said:

"Redefine the definition of Wealth. Instead of seeing wealth as a "number"', see it as a period of time. Determine wealth by how long you could survive without you (or anyone in your household) physically working. For example, if all your bills and expenses totaled $5,000 per month and you have $20,000 in savings, your wealth would be 4 months because that's how long you could maintain without an income."

I forever had a new definition of wealth and a new way of viewing the money I had. If I spend $25 a week on commissary and have $100 on my account, my wealth was only 4 weeks. I began to imagine how I could expand my wealth into years and decades which helped me see a larger picture.

When setting goals, always make them SMART:

Specific
Measurable
Action-oriented

Realistic
Timely

Life is a continuous struggle. Success requires sacrifice and discipline. These are universal principles, NOT opinions. Facts. Knowing these things, is success something you truly desire? Do you understand what it means to desire something?

You can ask anyone on your gallery and they're all gonna say they desire to become millionaires. Some may dream bigger and say they wanna be billionaires! But each and every day you watch them take no steps to achieve this desire. So the question becomes, do people truly want the things that they think/say they want? Do they know them selves enough to accurately describe what it really is they want from life? At this point, probably not.

When somebody truly desires something, this desire becomes their "organizing principle". Every action and thought will stem from the seed of this desire and each day will work towards its manifestation. This is the magic of desire and the power of the mind. Desire is the seed, the mind is the soil - plant it and it will grow. You'll be able to see it grow. Therefore, how many people around us actually have the seeds of desire planted within the soil of their mind? How many people seem to have some unbreakable force pushing them in a specific direction?

The same people who claim to want to be millionaires but make no daily effort to become one have no actual idea of what it takes to maintain millions of dollars. They don't understand the work, discipline, and effort required from people who have achieved success. Once they understand it, would they still desire it? Probably not.

You see, people just imagine some feeling of happiness or some life at ease that they believe instantly comes from success, but they're mistaken. Have they forgotten, or not truly realize, that with more money comes more problems? If you can't handle the problems you face today, what makes you think you can handle more problems? Problems that are much more complex than they currently face? It's a lie that people have come to believe, something they reaffirm within themselves every day." "All I need is (amount of money) and then I'll be straight!" Any of us that have ever said that before- and actually reached the goal - know that we're never "Straight" at this point. We didn't instantly find happiness and life didn't suddenly become easy.

I shake my head as I watch the amount of effort a person puts in to get some K2 every day, or to play somebody on the phone out of some money-but put no effort into what it actually takes to achieve one's goals. This is when I have to sit back and reflect on the reality of the situation -

these ARE people's goals. Getting high to escape the moment and using people for their money. These are their goals, their true desire, their organizing principle, because we can see the actions taken to achieve them. Any belief outside of this is a person's lack of self-knowledge. People repeat what they think they're supposed to say, and then come to believe that they desire these things they've been programmed to say - but this is only an illusion of the mind, a trance that we have placed ourselves under.

Most people truly desire a life of ease, enough "entertainment" to numb their thought process, and a considerable amount of happiness. And that is 100% okay - but it is a mistake to equate these things with financial wealth. Financial success requires the opposite of these things. The goals of most people could be achieved within a state of poverty because most of those things are mental. You just need to organize your mind.

Whatever it is you're trying to get from your life, whatever it is you truly desire, can only come after you've cleaned out your mind and organized it. De-clutter what's going on inside your brain by replacing television and music with reading and meditating. Reflect on your past, not to "Reminisce on the good times" but to travel through the darkness and understand why you are the way you are. What traumas do you suffer from?

Everybody suffers from trauma, and trauma dictates most of our compulsive behaviors that we don't understand.

There's a lot going on inside your mind. With all this free time we have as prisoners, put in some effort to clean out your closet and get your shit together. You're a powerful conscious being - you have it inside of you to get control over yourself. If you don't develop the discipline to control yourself, how can you control anything else - such as your business, organization, a family unit? Becoming a man begins with taking responsibility for your actions, gaining control over your emotions, and being honest with yourself. Always remember that being a member of the male species doesn't always make one a man. And the same thing applies to women and the other members of the female species.

Want a life of continuous education, effort, sacrifice, heavy thinking, healthy living - happiness? If so, start all these things today. If you don't, financial success isn't something that you truly desire. And there's nothing wrong with that. Everything is not for everybody. But begin to organize your mind and recognize that the things you truly desire are available if only you alter your mindset and attitude. You don't have to want something just because everybody else wants it (or thinks they want it).

Everybody wants to have a million dollars, but most people don't actually desire to be a millionaire. Being a millionaire is a way of life, a mental attitude manifested as action. People who want to have a million dollars want it to spend, to blow it on things that entertain them enough to not have to think or put any effort into life. But what happens when the million dollars is gone? Back to square one again, hoping somebody drops another million bucks in their hand and mad at the world if it doesn't happen. And this is the same thing with your freedom. Everyone wants the world to mysteriously open the doors for us - without us putting any effort into deserving the doors to be opened – and will remain mad at the world when it never happens. If we truly desire our freedom, our actions will back our desires.

People won't like what I'm about to say but I have to speak on what I believe - if your daily actions don't back your desire for freedom, you don't truly desire your freedom. You're confused about what you truly desire, and "freedom" is the simplest answer without having to do too much self-reflection. True desire is ALWAYS backed by action, by effort. It is within desire's nature to do so and cannot be otherwise. Anything else isn't true desire. There's no such thing as "I truly desire my freedom but I don't want to work for it". That's not a real thing and whoever believes this (or lives like this) is at odds with themselves. They're struggling with their own mind. And we've all been there before. This is why I'm saying that you must organize your mind. Without doing so, you will remain at odds with yourself.

Drugs

I had just finished writing the chapter on "Organize Your Mind" when my cell door slid open on the automatic puller system. It was time for me and my group of 30 people to get our 3-hours out in the day room. I associate with a few of the guys I've known for some time that are in my group. One of the guys was my cellie a few years back so I know his character pretty well. The disappointing conversation we had that afternoon didn't come as a surprise but it's the exact mode of thinking that this book was wrote to attack against. We were eating dinner after our workout, waiting for our commissary to get here, when he says to me "Man, mutha fuckas bout to be mad at me this week because I'm not payin' em nothin'? They gon have to catch up with me." This guy clearly has a vice - a k2 habit

- and is attempting to have his cake and eat it too. I asked him how much he owed, and he responded. "I owe 60 and I only got 100 coming. That's damn near the whole bag! They can't have that." I immediately responded with "They can have that, you just don't want to come off it. You could pay it, you're just choosing not to." He started laughing and said "Yeah, basically. They just gon have to catch up with me." Because I've seen this thing happen thousands of times, it wasn't anything new to me but I still had to tell him "You ain't right". I just had to let him know and make sure he knows he's wrong for his train of thought, hoping he won't act upon it. He says, "How I ain't right? Mutha fuckas do it to me all the time! Plus, they ain't gonna do nothin' about it - they know I can fight."

Typical to my character, I explained to him how this shit isn't about how other people act or what other people have done in the past. I told him he's supposed to be the change he wants to see in the world, to hold himself to a higher standard. Do you think that just because people tell on me that Ima tell on people? - No. This isn't about treating others how they treat you - that philosophy would ding us all down to the lowest common denominators very fast (and we're not communists). If you believe in something, you stand on it. As a man, standing on principle doesn't depend on whether other people stand on it or not. As a man, you do what you believe is right even if everyone else believes you're wrong. Be the guy that others want to be like, not the one that every one stays away from.

He goes on to say how they "ain't gunna do nothin' about it -they know I can fight" and I said that has nothing to do with it. I explained it's about the principle - it's principle that we're standing on. Do you believe in paying your debts? - if the answer is "yes" then pay all of your debts.If the answer is "no", then don't pay any of your debts. But the worst thing you could do is "pick and choose" who you're going to pay depending on their "threat level". This mentality shows nothing but fear and cowardice. If you're gonna pay this guy his $10 because you know he'll stab you if you don't, but you don't even believe in paying your debts - what does this say about you. It says you pay because you fear the outcome - NOT because you're a man of integrity. That's not a good look for someone to have in here or out there. When you choose to NOT pay someone because you know the particular person won't sweat you over $10, or over $100, you're fucking up the game for everybody and making us look bad as a people. How can we come together to fight against our oppressors if we can't trust each other? We can't.

This is one of the things I hate about drugs - the fact that they diminish moral character and change the things you care about. A man of integrity can quickly fall out of grace after developing a drug habit. I've seen it over and over as it happens all the time. But I really despise the fact that these drugs are <u>meant for us</u>, designed to destroy us and our dignity, pushed into our communities by the people who aim to oppress us. We know these things, we know what they do to us - but we still use them. We still push them.

To be clear, the pushers are no better off than the users from the view of "what" is destroying communities and oppressing people. Pushers depend on the users, so if you look in the mirror and say "I'm better than them because I don't use that shit. I just sell it". - you're lying to yourself. You would be nothing without them; you need them to smoke up all this product that destroys the family unit. Your success depends on the amount of destruction they (you) are causing.

Now, I'm not saying there is any thing inherently wrong about selling drugs - after all, people are "free" (technically) to choose whether or not they wanna use it. And if you don't provide it, someone else will anyway, maybe even the government (as they already do). And you need that money. I get it, I really do. I was in that lane my whole life and I struggle every day to stay out of it. Hustling is my addiction - making something out of nothing, a quarter out a nickel. I love that shit, I love that feeling-and a junkie loves how that dope feels.

If you really step back and look at the game objectively, if you can be honest with yourself - when you're hustling, it's that feeling that you're addicted to. It's that lifestyle that comes with it, and the fact that after you've made $100,000 in 30 days it no longer makes sense to work a 9 to 5 for $40,000 a year... Everything has changed within your brain once-you've really got into the hustling game, and a normal life will never appear the same no more. That 9 to 5 life is too slow, it's too boring. There's not enough color and excitement - it's too gray. No, there's no going back to that way of living - hustling is your new lifestyle. BUT - <u>what you need to look in the mirror and understand</u> - this is a <u>feeling</u> you're addicted to <u>in the exact same way the user is addicted to the drug</u>. It's the <u>feeling</u> they're addicted to. It's the <u>lifestyle</u> that comes with it, and the fact that after you've been having the best sex of your life for 4 hours straight, normal 30-minute sober sex just doesn't do the same trick...Everything has changed within your brain once you've really started using drugs, and a normal life will never appear the same no more. That 9 to 5 life is too slow, it's too boring. There's not enough color and excitement - it's too gray. No, there's no going back to that way of living – drug using is your new lifestyle.

But, at the very least, the drug user is <u>aware</u> this is a matter of addiction and is honest with themself about it, whereas the drug seller is <u>oblivious</u> to the fact of there being no real difference between the two activities. Both activities create a false sense of objective reality, they both are destructive to the brain, both are destructive to the community and the family unit. They are both dependent upon each other - and they are both weapons used by the oppressors with the premeditated intent of causing <u>all the above</u> to us as a class of people.

I'm not a drug addict or a drug user - I'm not taking sides in this debate. I'm trying to help the hustlers see how (if you're honest with yourself) you're not much different than the user, and you're no "better" than them either. You need them, as they need you, and you both suffer from a feeling that you're addicted to. What's really interesting to consider is how the only real difference between the two is subjective...

It comes down to pride, ego, and whether or not you care about another person's opinion of you. Let's say that you don't care about people's opinions and that you've gotten over your pride - one hit of dope provides you the same feeling (if not better) that the hustlers feel after every successful run...except hustlers risk "life in prison" and a loss of everything they've gained, whereas the user risks nothing but a drug ticket. A fine.

As hustlers, we tend to negatively judge those who use drugs - but are they smarter than us? Have they made the smarter, more precautious decision amongst the two paths of destruction? All they've got to do is take a hit - and heaven comes to them. We have to chase heaven, while avoiding being shot, robbed, killed, and indicted. But we all have the same goal - enjoying a piece of heaven. We just view differently what heaven looks like from within our own minds, but the feeling is the same. Heaven feels like heaven, and we're addicted to it. As players of the same game, the only difference between us is which path we have chosen to receive our piece of Heaven.

Hustlers - remember, the lifestyle that a user lives may appear unattractive to us, but it's not unattractive to them. In their minds, they are in heaven. Just as in your mind, you are too. The only people who are truly hurting by these actions are those members of our family and our community who are not part of the game but suffer as a result of our own selfish decisions, our own addictions. The only people who benefit are the oppressors.

Know your Self. What do you care about outside of yourself? Do you care about freedom? Do you care about better communities and safer neighborhoods for our loved ones? Do you care about providing a better education to our children and better opportunities throughout their lives? Do you care about overcoming our oppression? Or- do you only care about the feeling you receive from the lifestyle you've chosen - and fuck everything else? These things cannot coincide with each other. There can be no compromise between food and poison - death will always win.

It all boils down to knowing what you truly, genuinely care about- what you truly desire. And you have to know thyself in order to know what it is you care about, believe in, and stand upon. A person's actions always reflect what it is they truly care about. The words that spill from their mouths mean nothing when their actions don't match. Anyone who sells dope cannot truly care about their community and the bettering of the people. It's contradictive. It's not a belief that has been determined after allowing one's thought process to unravel all the kinks in the lifestyle and what it actually entails. Rather, "bettering" our community is something they claim to be about because they think that's what they're supposed to say. They think that's what they're supposed to believe in - but, if they genuinely believed in these things, would they indulge in a way of living that actively opposes this belief? Of course not. Would a genuine Muslim choose to skip prayers and eat pork on a regular basis? Of course not - because their belief within their religion is genuine. Their actions reflect their belief. Their belief system has caused them to refrain from actions that oppose their goal.

What do you believe in?

What do your actions reflect that you believe in?

Do your beliefs even matter if your actions oppose them?

Really take some time to think about the way we've been living. Meditate for awhile. Turn off the TV and try to work through some of the thoughts going through your head. Don't play any music with lyrics in it. Just think, with no distractions. What is it that you genuinely care about? What is it that you believe in? What do you want? Is freedom the actual goal?

I believe that freedom is always the goal - has always been the goal-for you and for me. I just think we're all suffering from addictions and traumas, human tragedies, that have left our mind clouded, unable to see how our actions aren't matching the things we believe in.

Going back to the story about dude not trying to pay his debts – I know that somewhere inside of him he actually believes that paying his debts is the right thing to do, and that he cares about doing the right thing. I think that life has beaten him down so badly, he's beginning to lose pieces of himself. He's beginning to forget who he is and who he wants to be. Every day he wakes up to face a sentence of 50-70 years and everybody around him wakes up miserable, mad at the world and hating everybody in it. It doesn't help that most of these miserable people around him are serving less than half the time that he's serving but even they can't find any reason to be happy.

Everybody in here wakes up searching for a way to escape their reality and he's becoming a product of this environment. He's becoming exactly what this environment was designed to produce - a broken spirit. A lost hope. A negative attitude. Envy, sadness, jealousy, anger, regret, despair. I wake up every morning hoping to inspire positivity and light, hoping that I can discover a method by which people don't fall victim to this machine that tears us apart. And as of right now, I don't know how to spread the mental program from one mind to the next. I don't know how to let it sink in that there is a different way to live from inside of here, that there is still a way to be happy. And until I discover a method to adequately share the message, I can only be the change that I want to see in the world - and hope the flame catches wind.

As can you - men of integrity

Reason, Season, or Lifetime

People come into your life for a reason, a season, or a lifetime.

When you figure out which one it is,

you will know what to do for each person.

*When someone is in your life for a **Reason**,*

It is usually to meet a need you have expressed.

They have come to assist you through a difficulty;

provide you with guidance and support;

to aid you physically, emotionally or spiritually-

They may seem like a godsend, and they are.

They are there for the reason you need them to be.

Then, without any wrongdoing on your part or at an inconvenient time,

this person will say or do something to bring the relationship to an end.

Sometimes they die. Sometimes they walk away.

Sometimes they act up and force you to take a stand.

What we must realize is that our need has been met, our desire fulfilled;

their work is done.

The prayer you sent up has been answered and now it is time to move on.

*Some people come into your life for a **Season***

because your turn has come to share, grow or learn.

They bring you an experience of peace to make you laugh.

They may teach you something you have never done.

They usually give you an unbelievable amount of joy.

Believe it. It is real. But only for a season.

***Lifetime** relationships teach you lifetime lessons;*

things you must build upon in order to have a solid emotional foundation.

Your job is to accept the lesson, love the person,

And put what you have learned to use

in all other relationships and areas of your life.

It is said that love is blind but friendship is clairvoyant.

-Unknown

Friends

Friends... how many of us have them?

I've always heard people talk about there being a difference between friends and homies. This really had me thinking so I decided to look up what the American Heritage dictionary defines "friend" to be.

Friend- a person whom one knows, likes, and trusts. (emphasis I included)

Trust- firm belief in the integrity or ability of a person or thing.

Well damn... if a friend is a person I know, like, and trust then what does that make a "homie"? The American Heritage dictionary doesn't have a definition for that one.... maybe I'll ask Google.

We've all heard people say phrases similar to this one: "He's the homie but I don't really fuck with him like that." This usually means he's from your hood or yal have some form of alliance but you either don't like him or trust him- one of the two. So, we could almost define a homie as someone "you fuck with because you're stuck with". But this don't apply to every case so there's gotta be a further definition of what a homie is. Someone might not even be from your hood but he's still the homie - although you wouldn't consider him your friend. Is the term "homie" one of respect, a title you give to someone whom you may not even like but you've given your loyalty to based on his reputation? I see that kind of thing all the time as well, where you know this dude don't like that dude but he still calls him "the homie". What does this all mean and what are we even doing?

As people mature and grow, there comes a time when they realize that this gang shit is for the birds; there's no longer the honor and loyalty in it like there was supposed to be. Principles have slowly disintegrated, and we begin to notice gang ties as nothing but restrictions we've placed on ourselves that stop us from networking with other people except who we "fuck with because we're stuck with " - not necessarily people whom we'd consider to be our friends or good business associates. Of course, some of them may be, but if they're real friends then they'd be your friend with or without gang ties.

This chapter is not me at all telling people to "drop their flags" or to allow themselves to get x'd out. No, never place your integrity or reputation at risk. I'm asking people to see these gang ties for what they are - restrictions and limitations, imprisoning you to your neighborhood.

There's nothing wrong with having pride in your neighborhood or love for where you came from, but if we allow this gang shit to cloud our vision from seeing the bigger picture, we're allowing our oppressors to win. Our oppressors love when we're on gang time, or when tension remains high between gangs and races. Divide and conquer. That's a real thing, that's a real strategy them people use to keep us in our place. We can't keep allowing these people to defeat us with the oldest trick in the book. That'd be like letting someone you play in chess beat you every single game with that same four-move- checkmate! You don't let a guy checkmate you with the same moves because you (1) saw what was going on, and (2) made adaptations in your strategy that stop it from continuing.

This is the kind of strategy that we've got to apply in real life. It does us no good to know what's going on if we fail to apply what we know. And we all know that gang time is overrated, we know it's counter productive to the war we truly face... So what are we doing? I understand the need for "cars" in prison, I understand the need for politics and policing your own people - and that determining your own people is through gang divisions, race, or religion. Human beings are the most powerful animals on the planet for many reasons, one of them because we possess the ability to discriminate. It's natural to our species to discriminate amongst each other, to recognize that we are different from each other. That is fine because we are all different and it's okay to discriminate. To "discriminate" means to make a clear distinction; differentiate. (American Heritage). I discriminate all the time, just not based upon race, religion, or gang ties. We're always going to discriminate in some way but this doesn't mean we should turn against one another or declare the other as the enemy because they're different. Recognizing our differences and then working together within them would make the best strategy in life and in the war we've been forced to fight.

The most important film of this last decade is *"Judas and the Black Messiah"* - the story of Fred Hampton's attempt to unite the proletariats (lower class people of all races) and overthrow our oppressors. He was murdered at the young age of 21 by our government officials. This is not a conspiracy theory - this was a real conspiracy by the F.B.I. to murder a revolutionary, a fact they have admitted to and had to pay for in civil court. They were never held criminally liable for the premeditated murder they admitted to committing which shows just how real and powerful our enemy is. It's hard to fight an enemy who has no face, no place to target - which is why our one and only defense against these attacks is the unity of all prisoners, the unity of all poor people of any race. The unity of the people.

(The F.B.I. government program that was created for infiltrating and destroying revolutionary movements was called COINTELPRO. This was a real thing, and probably still is a thing - just under a different name or no name at all. Remember: invisible enemy).

I am not a communist or a socialist, and I understand this whole "unity of the people" sounds like propaganda straight out of *"The Communist Manifesto"*. I am a capitalist- through and through- but capitalism is a dream and a goal, one which has never been achieved. Capitalism translates to freedom, a concept America has never seen. It's easy to blame capitalism and capitalists for the problems in our country, *as* the problem with our country, but the problem can never be with freedom. The problem is what people chose to do with their freedom. Communist dictator Lenin once asked *"Freedom to do what?"* He (as do all communist sympathizers) understands that people are not responsible enough as a whole to have freedom without self-destruction (as is with our gangs, on the lower level of politics). They will abuse their freedoms and become tainted by it. The underlying nature of communism/socialism is the oppression of the people's freedom. I understand and believe in the power of unity, but we can unite <u>without becoming</u> socialists or communists. We can unite while being free-but, like everything else in freedom, it comes down to a choice. Communism <u>forces</u> people to unite, but I see <u>uniting by choice</u> as a much more beautiful <u>and powerful </u>method.

One's moral character and integrity can only be judged by the choices a person makes <u>when not forced to make them</u>. Would all the "law abiding citizens" still obey the laws if there was no punishment for disobeying them? Would people drive at a reasonable speed if there was no speeding limit in place? Would people still pay taxes if they didn't have to? Would they still choose to live the same way they do now if there was no law in place that prohibits them? Do you believe people wouldn't take whatever they desired from stores without paying if there was no punishment or social ridicule? Would these same people who kill animals for sport NOT kill a man they hate during a heated argument if there was no possibility of punishment (including spiritual)? Maybe, maybe not, but we do know that these law-abiding citizens would act differently if there was no law to abide by. Their fear of whatever punishment comes from violating a law is what keeps them "law-abiding" - not necessarily because they agree with it. Fear- the same emotion used to control the masses within communist nations, fascist countries, and the gang life. Oppression.

I repeat it again: *one's moral character and integrity can only be judged by the choices a person makes when not forced to make them. When fear is what dictates our actions, we are oppressed. We are not free.*

When our morals determine the choices we make, there would be no need for a law to "keep us in place". Again, if men were angels there would be no need for the government. Morals are self-determined laws and ways of living that we follow as a guide because we believe in them as principles of righteousness- not because we fear a punishment. We desire to be righteous. We've thought about and reflected upon why each moral is of a righteous nature and have made the personal decision to live a moral life because we are a moral people (or, working to become them).

We are not born with morals; they are something we develop throughout life's experiences. The unthinking person, and most law-abiding citizens, adopt their morals based on what is legal or illegal within their residence. They believe that without the law none of us would know what our morals are supposed to be. That's bullshit, and an excuse for mental laziness.

Morals are not developed or recognized by knowing what your government has declared to be legal; morals come through reflection. The central tenet that Jesus taught to the people was a guide for us to use while determining what is moral - the message to treat others in the way that you would like to be treated. Sounds simple enough, but rarely is it reflected upon or abided by as a guide. Living a moral life requires knowing and being honest with yourself.

When determining whether an action or belief is moral, ask yourself "How would I feel if this same action I'm about to take were to be taken against me?" After being honest with yourself, if the act or belief would not affect you or hurt you- it can be determined moral.

This task requires empathy and a basic understanding of human emotions, in general. We're not all the same exactly but for the most part we are. Empathy doesn't come naturally (note how selfish little children usually are) but if you can learn how to care for others, or at least have a respect for them, you can be a moral person.

Treating others how you would like to be treated is the easiest way to live a moral life. If you always ask yourself and answer honestly whether you would like it if the same thing were happening to you, the answer to "what is moral?" becomes pretty simple. However simple it may seem; it does require maturity and responsible reasoning skills.

After knowing what is moral, if everyone made a conscious decision to live a moral life - to treat others how they'd like to be treated — there would be no need for law. There would be no need for government. The only reason that law and government exist is because people don't treat others how they'd like to be treated. But - imagine if we did! Imagine a society where everybody treated others with respect and chose to act in accordance with morals. This would be a place with no law, no violence, no oppression. A place of harmony. But most importantly, it would be a place wherein the soul of each person can be judged to be moral, to be righteous – because they chose to be! This place would be Heaven, right here on earth. We would all be friends with each other, or at least trust each other.

Develop your moral integrity by treating others how you would like to be treated. Don't justify your actions by thinking "I know he'd do it to me so Ima do it to him. This concept breeds immoral actions and instills the need for a government to oversee our behavior. Cut it out. As Ghandi put it, *"Be the change you want to see in the world."* To me, this quote is a more developed version of "treat others how you'd like to be treated" because it asks you to imagine the ideal you have for humanity and then become that person. It inspires growth and advises you to lead by example. But the goal is the same.

If you become a responsible person, there is no need for someone else (ie. government) to tell you what you can or can't do. No responsible person needs any agency to dictate their decisions. We understand we have the God-given privilege to do anything we want - long as we don't violate the freedoms of others.

Freedom - I don't care what you do in this world or with your life, just don't hurt anybody. Life can be simple as that; in fact, it is meant to be simple as that. But sadly, we have fallen from grace.

The dream of a true republic is a land where everybody is responsible and no government is needed. Ahhhh... the smell of freedom is making my eyes run.

It all begins with a choice - a choice that each of us must make to treat others how we'd like to be treated. Then, and only then, can we be liberated. I mean... unless you like being in prison. Unless you like the feeling of missing a woman, of missing out on what life has to offer. If you like that shit, if you don't hate the prison system, continue being destructive. But if you're tired of this shit and desire freedom more than anything else -

you now know what is required of you to achieve it. You no longer have any excuse or justification for your destructive behaviors. It's all on you and the boulder isn't that difficult to carry.

What does this all have to do with the idea of friendship? - Everything. The "friend" is someone you know, like, and trust. A friend is the ideal that each of us should aim to become - knowable, likable, trustable. What has surprised me over the years is how many different people have approached me and said "You know, I see you in a different light than I see guys around here. You're a good person and you really don't deserve to be here…You're one of the only people I can actually call a friend." Initially when I'd hear statements similar to this from all these different people, I would think "I barely spend any time with this person…. how can he see me as a friend?" My paranoid self would think they were just ego stroking and maybe had a hidden agenda (some of them did). Throughout the years I'd find myself wishing I had a clone in here with me as a partner because I couldn't trust anybody... but everybody trusted me. My desire to have another version of myself caused me to reflect upon myself - what is it that attracts all these different people to me? What is it about myself that is different than others in here? None of these reflections were egocentric questions, genuinely trying to figure out what was going on. And this is when I discovered the power of integrity!

Integrity was the one and only thing that separates me (and other men of integrity) from others - that one, four syllable, nine letter word. But, this one word entails a world of difference between those with it and those without it. My integrity is what caused people to see me as "a good person who doesn't deserve to be here, a friend". This is how we need society to view us... good people that don't need to be in prison; friends. There can be no friendship without trust. What's the easiest way to develop trust from a large amount of people? - always treat others how you would like to be treated. I don't want that done to me so I'm not going to do it to them. It sounds so simple - and it turns you into a friend.

Rather than dreaming of some communist/socialist state where each of us are forced into the lowest common denominator out of fear, why not preach the power of friendship? Of what it means to be a good friend, not just to a group of people or a gang or a country, but to all of humanity. You don't have to be religious to become a genuine person, and it means more when you do it out of the goodness of your soul.

When you're forced into acting like a good person, you're really not a good person. You're suppressing emotions and actions because you're forced to, looking for any way to express them and escape this force. The same concept applies to racism and what we see going on right now in our daily lives. With the civil rights movements and the approval of affirmative action in the 60's and 70's, racist people were forced to act like they weren't racist. Did this mean these people actually quit being racist and healed their souls? Of course not, we've seen the explosion of the last 50 years of suppressed racism in the rise of Donald Trump. When you're forced into acting like a good person, movies like The Purge become appealing to you. Like... what?

Jesus is the archetype of the "friend". Judas is the archetype of the "betrayer". The betrayer is one who violates trust. If you are not worthy of trust, you are a Judas. It's imperative that we see the flaws in our character and the error of our ways. Especially as prisoners. People in the free world suffer from these flaws as well and it's just as necessary for them to develop integrity but we're literally imprisoned for it and will continue to suffer until we can prove our integrity (as a whole) to the world.

Right now, citizens of the world see no problem with the prison system and some even see it to be "too weak" on criminals. This is because they don't want to be surrounded by Judas... but who of us do? I don't want to live in a world where I can't trust my neighbors, neither do they. Free people see us as the lowest of the low because that's what we are. Don't look in the mirror and lie to yourself about it. Look in the mirror and be honest. "Yes, I've done some fucked up things in my life. Because of the things I've done, I'm a member of the lowest of the low. This is an objective fact. I don't want to remain in this position; therefore, I will grow into a higher being. I will set out to become the best version of myself."

When freedom is the goal, there is no other option. Becoming the highest version of yourself is one of the only purposes we have within this experience called life. The highest version of yourself can see the bigger picture, can see what the oppressors are doing to us, and will work to unite all prisoners rather than divide and turn us amongst each other.

We are all different. Yes. Clearly, we have our differences, but differences shouldn't make us enemies. If anything, our differences are what help us learn from each other. But we're playing right into these people's plans when we hate each other based on race, religion, politics, gangs. We fall into their hands when we hate each other at all, for whatever reason. To hate someone, you must have an emotional connection to them. Whatever you hate, you ultimately care about in some way. Rather than hate, it's easier and healthier to understand and ignore.

I used to hate these C.O.'s until I realized I'm giving them way too much energy, thought, and control over myself. I had to understand that most of them are people who have made nothing of themselves within their own lives, are probably just as bitter as we are because of it, and choose to target us to make themselves feel better. Others are here simply to do their job and nothing else, some just want the easy paycheck. Ignore these people's little tantrums. Don't take any of it personally. They don't even know you so it can't be personal.

In prison, we must always expect "shake downs" and expect "misconduct reports" if we're caught violating the rules. Don't lose your cool when it happens. Be prepared for it. If you get caught slippin' you can only be mad at yourself. Being mad at the C.O.'s for doing their job (even when they're doing the most and being petty) is only going to keep you mad forever.

There was this one incident a few years back when I was so upset after an officer busted me that I was ready to explode! He had went over and beyond any measure I've ever seen an officer take before in order to catch somebody and I was losing my mind because of it. I didn't know how to handle my anger and I was so pissed because I got caught. As he's taking me to a holding cell while I'm handcuffed behind my back, I'm calling him every derogatory term I could think of, hoping my words would hurt him in any way... but this dude responded with a statement that changed my life. He said, "*Look... it's my job to catch you breaking the rules. It's your job to not let me catch you. Don't be mad at me because I'm doing my job better than you're doing yours.*"...and nothing was the same.

In that moment it hit me. He was right and I couldn't even argue with him. I would never be mad at somebody for doing their job again. I can only respect it. I'm going to make sure that I'm the best at my job and we're just gonna battle it out like that. If I wanted to continue breaking the rules then I was gonna be the best at what I do. This view made it all seem like a game to me, a survival contest between who's more fit for their job, which helped alleviate the feelings of hate from my body.

Don't get me wrong - there's still a thick line between us and them. I'm well aware they're soldiers of our oppressors but most of them are too concerned with their own daily lives to even see who it is they're working for and what it is that they're doing to us. They're pawns in the game - we're bishops, knights, and rooks... focused on the checkmate. Don't focus your hatred on the pawns when you're bigger than that. We're all bigger than that.

One of the dreams I have would be if every prisoner were to become a man of integrity, were to treat each other as friends in some way, and eliminate our violent and negative ways of life - the human goodness within the hearts of the guards would cause them to empathize with us, to see the injustice going on in the criminal justice system, and become a voice for us out there in the world! Imagine that, the guards becoming our voice. The pawns of our oppressors turning against our oppressors- this would create a serious ripple effect in the system. People would listen to them. People would believe them. Prison reform would be a much easier battle if the guards believed the system was cruel or unfair. But right now, these people come to work and see us as animals - wild animals. They come every day prepared for violence because that's what we show them. They witness their co-workers being assaulted by us, treated disrespectfully, and it appears that we have no respect for human life.

The way things currently are, there's no hope for any of them to believe we deserve freedom or feel that we're being mistreated. Most guards now believe we deserve exactly what we're getting, probably even more now than when they first started working for corrections. And that doesn't help us at all. If the guards are saying to the world, "Hell no, you better not let those people out here with us! If you could only see how they act..." then our chances of ever receiving support from society become lower. But imagine if they were saying the opposite - if they were showing up in groups to speak with congress, fighting to free us from our imprisonment! Or, because of their empathy for us, imagine if they all came together to strike- refusing to go to work any more until light was shed on the injustices and things were changed! Just imagine. There's already a shortage of officers across the nation; they couldn't just fire everybody and rehire. They can barely keep enough staff as it is.

This won't ever happen - but it could happen. It's not impossible... if we could all see the bigger picture and work to achieve it. Unity amongst us. Being a friend instead of a homie.. Treating others with the respect we'd like to receive. This is all possible, and this is all it would take. If there's a will to bring every one together under this light, there's a way to achieve it. Ultimately you only have power over your self and your own actions. Make the decision for your self to treat others with respect because everybody needs a friend. Being a man of integrity is value, something rare, but is a requirement of true freedom. We've got a long ways to go as a unit, but it all gotta start somewhere.

"Understand, the people we served were at the bottom of the socioeconomic ladder, their existences unrecognized. Prisoners had never had their name anywhere except in relation to a crime, and that's nothing to be proud of. The prison employees were basically the same. The only thing distinguishing many from the prisoners they guarded was the color of the uniforms they wore. Nobody goes to school dreaming of becoming a prison guard. They're there because, like the prisoners, the circumstances of their lives conspired against them, causing them to end up in prison. And, like prisoners, they get very little respect from society. But that creates an opportunity for a publication that recognizes and serves the world of the keeper and the kept, humanizing those who live, work, achieve, struggle,

suffer, and die in it. Do a good job of it, and they'll support you. That's

power." - Wilbert Rideau

PART TWO

SYO Business

Job opportunities are pretty limited these days as technology advances and the divide between the 1% and the rest of us widens... and that's without being a felon. Being a felon puts an entirely different restriction on us and makes finding a meaningful career difficult. Don't get me wrong, a male felon will always have opportunities such as physical labor and construction, and may even receive a decent pay check for it. But our goal in life is not to be trapped in the caste system. The wear and tear of our bodies causes wear and tear to our minds, spirit, and emotions. It's not something we can continue doing into our elderly years. There's nothing wrong with working but why work for someone else when we can do the same thing they do?

As felons we're still allowed to legally own our choice of businesses, real estate, and franchises. We're still allowed to be the bosses that we naturally are and these are opportunities that we must take advantage of. The mindset must always be "Why work at a McDonalds *when I can own* a McDonalds?" This must be how we train ourselves to think. We must educate ourselves to become business owners.

No form of real material wealth will ever come to us as worker bees. Good jobs that make someone rich are barred from us. But, after transforming our hustle, we can still become rich as business owners. Everything you do in the business world or work place should be inspired by the thought "How can I do this myself?" or "How can I own this myself?"

Using McDonalds as an example, let's say I'm fresh out of prison and have no car and I need a job and there's a McDonalds two blocks away. Hell yeah you better go get that job there, but treat your work as a learning experience. Learn exactly what it takes to make a McDonalds operate and master every job yourself, every position. Tell yourself I'm going to own a McDonalds someday so it's best I know how to do every job inside here. Use your job as the means to an end, but never the end itself. The end game is personal ownership - is sitting at home doing whatever you want as your "personally owned" McDonalds is running like a well-greased machine bringing you in over 10 bands profit a month. From doing nothing. Purchase and expand. That's what we're on just like that's what they're on. The rich get richer because they got the money to buy shit up; most of us grow up not even knowing that the goal is to buy shit up.

Public education doesn't teach you what you need to know about business or real estate, not even the basics, nor the correct way to view money. Public education teaches you how to become a "worker bee" (starting by placing you inside a "factory" called school for 8-hours a day, Monday through Friday, the first 13 years of your life). Without parents who knew better, we only learned about money and business by what our schools taught (basically nothing). If you've never heard of the book *"Rich Dad, Poor Dad"* by Robert Kiyosaki, it is highly recommended because it introduces the different business/money educations we receive as children depending on whether our parents were rich or poor (mentally). Robert Kiyosaki set out to educate people like us who didn't have a rich parent who could teach us the secrets to business, money, and success. Easy to read book. Inspirational, understandable, and life changing. Part two and three of his *"Rich Dad, Poor Dad"* series is called *"The Cashflow Quadrant"* and *"The Guide to Investing"*. These books, as well as other books published by Kiyosaki and his Rich Dad Advisers, are recommended reads for anyone trying to transform the way they see business ownership, and elevate their financial IQ. Ownership is required for anyone who desires to obtain generational wealth and provide an entirely different world for posterity.

"Personal ownership" is what America is all about. Capitalism is having the right to own personal property. Those who fuss most against capitalism are those who own nothing. Understand: communism/socialism are when the government owns everything and individuals are allowed to own nothing. Capitalism is the right of the individual to own his own things and do with them as he pleases. Capitalism is freedom to the individual, and if ownership is synonymous with freedom (the ultimate goal) then ownership must become a goal. Business and real estate ownership. That's what capitalism is all about and is the reason why America has prospered the way we have (so far). Freedom. Financial freedom.

Anything that you're interested in doing you can turn into your personally owned business. For example, I'm interested in writing- in spreading knowledge and stories (as well as obtaining them), in creating a difference in the world, and in helping other prisoners publish their own materials. Therefore I helped start a publishing company. BestSelf Publications is owned by my wife and a few members of her networking team which allows them the freedom to publish any/all of our material; whereas viewing my writing as a career from the mindset of a worker, I'd be dependent on other publishing companies to decide whether my work is worthy of being shared with the world or not. They would own my work and pay me what they believe it's worth - and that's cool, for the most part. It just isn't me, just isn't my style. I'm not gonna be submitting my manuscripts to all these different companies that are willing to offer me pennies when I can own the publishing company and make thousands. It's just not worth it to me to remain a worker anymore - unless I must.

One of my goals for BestSelf Publications was to free prisoner-writers from depending on major publishing companies to pick up their work for pennies. I want us to take matters into our own hands, making the most we possibly can from our projects, and get as much material in front of the world as we can to show that each and every one of us is More Than An Inmate. I work with other prisoners, as equals. -boss to boss. I don't seek to make others my employees. A rising tide raises all the boats. The goal of Best Self Publications is to "rise the tide" so that we all have a platform used to succeed.

The secret to maintaining these business relationships is to always think in terms of "win/win". What is the best possible deal we can devise where you walk away a winner and I walk away a winner. If we both come out of every business deal as winners, the tide rises and we'll always be open to doing business together again. Trust is developed. Empires are built this way.

"Win/Win is a frame of mind and heart that constantly seeks mutual benefit in all human interactions. Win/Win means that agreements of solutions are mutually beneficial, mutually satisfying. With a Win/Win solution, all parties feel good about the decision and feel committed to the action plan. Win/win sees life as a cooperative, not a competitive arena. Most people tend to think in terms of dichotomies: strong or weak, hardball or softball, win or lose. But that kind of thinking is fundamentally flawed. It's based on power and position rather than on principle. Win/Win is based on the paradigm that there is plenty for everybody, that one person's success is not achieved at the expense or exclusion of the success of others. Win/Win is a belief in the Third Alternative. It's not your way or my way; it's a better way, a higher way." - Stephen Covey

BestSelf Publications was inspired by the Win/Win attitude - there's a way that we can all win. And I'm willing to work with any character of integrity who is trying to work with me.

You notice that I said work "with" and not work for. Work, itself, will always be required. It's what you do with your work that matters. Turn your work into a business owned by you. And if your network hasn't grown to the extent that personal ownership is possible from behind bars, work with companies that possess a Win/Win mentality.

Even if you're not ready at this very moment to own your own, you're ready at this very moment to learn how to own your own and why you must.

By now I'm sure you've heard terms like "LLC" or "corporation" or "CEO" being thrown around in conversations, but what do these terms entail and what is all the hype about? It helps to understand "what" a corporation is and "why" they are important to the individual and our society by knowing how it was that corporations first began. In the 1500's English businesses were capitalizing from shipping products overseas to the New World (America). Supplies were placed on boats and shipped across the ocean in hopes of making it to America, where they would then turn a large profit. The problem was that not all the boats would make it across the seas without disappearing, by being robbed by pirates, natural disasters such as weather storms, etc — and taking major losses. The losses became so severe that companies began reconsidering whether it was a good idea to risk the investment of shipping products to America. If one of the shipments failed to deliver, people were held personally liable for the missing products and would have to pay for it using their own life's savings, their homes, and property. Companies would go from wealth to poverty overnight- which made people afraid to invest in America.

As companies began to fall back, America became desperate to receive supplies and products. The choice for England was between figuring out a less risky way to get products to America, OR, abandon America and forget about developing this New World. The only way companies continue to invest in these endeavors would be if they themselves were no longer personally liable for any potential disasters or losses they incur in the middle of the ocean.

Thus, the idea of the corporation was invented which ultimately meant that a business is treated as its own person and that only the business was liable for the failures - not the individuals who control it. This security net people now had over their own personal property and lives allowed companies to make investments in shipments again, but with much less risk. If it so happened that a boat would go down and all the merchandise disappears, only the corporation itself would be held liable, as its own entity. Only what the company owned could be paid out to suitors; all the property and money that the owners of the company possessed would be safe, protected by this shell called a corporation.

Corporations were invented to limit an investors risk AND to inspire risk-taking behavior. Without risks being taken, there can be no reward – no groundbreaking revolutionary changes or success. Things would always stay as they were. So, corporations inspire companies to take risks because the owner's personal assets are protected. It'd be like if you put a $15,000 down payment on a $100,000 car. You owe $85,000 for that vehicle. You wake up one morning and your car is gone, stolen, never to be seen again. You still owe $85,000 for this car and the creditors are coming for whatever little money you may have or property you may own and are destroying your credit score. But, had a corporation bought this car for $15,000 and lost it, who would be liable for this $85,000 debt? Not You (the owner of the corporation). The corporation itself would. Yes, the creditors are coming for whatever little money the corporation may have in its own account or whatever property it may own in its own name, and the creditors will destroy your corporations credit score - but your money and property and credit will remain safe, unharmed. What happens if the corporation can't pay its debt (or simply doesn't want to)? It files bankruptcy and all is forgotten. Game over. And what do you do after that? Start a new corporation again with a fresh start!

A corporation is a company with its own rights, its own credit history, its own bank account, its own assets, its own everything. It's like the company has a life of its own - even its own social security number (Tax Identity Number - TIN). The American Heritage dictionary defines a corporation as "an entity that is comprised of a body of persons but is legally sanctioned to operate as a single person, allowing it to enter into contracts and engage in transactions under its own identity."

The difference between opening your business and running it without incorporation is that without incorporation your business is you. It shares your credit, its bank account is separate but is still in your name, and if anything happens at your business, you are personally liable. Running a business like this-making up a name and getting a business license - is called a Sole Proprietorship. You're recognizing yourself as the owner of a business that you're liable for (you could lose your home and savings account if someone slips and falls at your job place).

But, if you have this same business but simply take the steps to incorporate it beforehand, you can no longer lose your home or savings if someone slips and falls. Incorporation equals protection. You still control your company once incorporated, you've just taken the necessary steps to protect yourself and your assets. Plus, the public is more trusting of a company that is incorporated under a structure. It appears more professional and credible.

There are several different structures that you can choose to incorporate your business under but the one I'll spend some space discussing (and recommending) is the Limited Liability Company - the LLC. It's a relatively new structure that allows you more freedoms and opportunities to organize your business however works for you and to run it how you please. The LLC isn't technically called a corporation but it's the same concept, and provides the same protections (if not more!). They are always mentioned when discussing options of incorporation. The difference between a corporation and a LLC is that a corporation is divided up by its owners into stocks/shares (which can be sold to investors), whereas the LLC is divided up into portions, using percentages. If four of us come together and decide to organize our business as an LLC and if we decide on equal ownership, we'd each own 25% of the company. This is the biggest difference between the LLC and a corporation (barely a difference at all).

The LLC structure is growing in popularity because it offers the same benefits as a corporate structure but is easy to operate and more fluid to organize. It's simply a better structure to use unless your company is going to be utilizing stocks/shares. In whatever case, if you dream of using stocks/shares at some point but your company isn't big enough yet, you can begin as a LLC and later restructure it into a corporation. It's not a problem.

As long as you recognize your LLC as an entity separate from yourself and treat it as such, you will never be personally liable for your companies' failures or lawsuits. If your company takes out a loan for $250,000 and fails to pay it back- long as you didn't back any loan with a personal guarantee - you are not responsible for your companies' debts. Rich people, such as Donald Trump before his silly ass got into politics, have taken large loans and ran their companies into the ground and you were not held personally liable for their bad business decisions (Imagine if you never held personally liable for your bad decisions, you'd never be in a prison cell).

If you've ever wondered how Trump was still a billionaire after he filed for bankruptcy, it's because he never personally filed for bankruptcy… His companies filed for bankruptcy. His companies failed and didn't have enough money to pay off the debt they'd incurred, and his bankruptcy pleadings allowed for all debt to be forgiven. Although this doesn't necessarily "look good" on your resume as business man- ultimately Trump's resume didn't matter... He never lost a personal penny and exploited the market.

You've probably heard a lot of nonsense from the news that claims "rich people don't pay taxes." As much as I dislike Trump and everything he stands for, I have to borrow his phrase to describe this phenomenon — fake news. If anybody in America does pay taxes, it's the rich people. What the news is attempting to explain is that many companies that rich people own don't pay taxes. True enough, and this is because these companies take advantage of the tax protections that LLC's and corporate structures are provided. It's not that successful companies refuse to pay taxes, therefore, are the bad guys. This is a terrible narrative that the media has pushed in order for politicians with a socialist agenda to pass laws against successful people. That's not a good plan for anybody, especially successful people.

In the same way that corporations were invented to inspire risk-taking and innovation, tax deductions were invented for the same purpose. Allowing companies to deduct the amount of taxes, one must pay for participating in specific activities inspires them to participate in specific activities. For example, donating money to a nonprofit organization is an activity that is tax deductible. Because nonprofit organizations generally benefit all of humanity, especially those in need, the IRS has told corporations "Hey, give some of your profits to the needy and, in exchange, we'll lower that amount from how much you're suppose to give to the government." This rule inspires people to donate more money than their good heart usually would to these organizations - which is a good thing for humanity and business men.

If the IRS gave you the option to either give your money to the government OR to give your money to any charity organization of your choice... most of us would give our money to a charity organization. Why wouldn't you? At least you'd have a sense of what your money is being spent on and you've maintained a choice in the matter (Especially because most of us don't agree with how the government chooses to spend our tax money).

Sounds reasonable enough... and this is a real thing. People who pay taxes are allowed this option, and all rich people use it. They'd much rather give to charity than to the government who, remind you, is trying to tear their companies apart. This is one method by which it appears rich people don't pay taxes.

Other tax deductive rules specifically inspire innovative behavior. Without the benefit of tax deductions, many companies may not have pursued projects that were risky but ultimately succeeded, changing the face of the world and making it a better place for everybody. One of these benefits is that companies can "write off" from their taxes any losses that their company has in the past. A large percent of companies actually lose money every year for the first five years and don't even begin to earn money until after a decade of business. A tax benefit that inspires these companies to keep pushing and not give up after the first few years of losses is that they can make some of this "lost money" back by not being forced to pay taxes on their profits. If you lose $100,000 in your first 5 years of business and then finally turn a profit, you're not forced to pay taxes until you've made back that $100,000. Until you've wrote off 100,000 of tax deductions, the IRS won't force you to pay taxes on your money.

This policy is reasonable to me, and inspirational to business owners, but is controversial to some people. Socialists don't like that in 2017 and 2018, Amazon legally paid little U.S. federal income taxes (even though they brought in over $10 billion in profits each of those years) because they're allowed to deduct historical losses against today's profits. But these policies have allowed Amazon to change the world and make each of our lives better - literally due to tax deductions for innovative behavior. Do you know that 75% of Americans trust Amazon more than they do the government? 51% of Americans go to church; 52% of Americans have Amazon Prime memberships! Shit is serious. If any transaction ever goes bad, Amazon will refund your money - even if the product was actually delivered and you just claim it wasn't! And how is Amazon able to refund people's money and ensure the best services to each of its customers? Because they're allowed to deduct from their taxes every refund they've ever given, documented as a company loss. Because of this tax deduction policy, Amazon gives away billions of dollars of products annually to its customers in exchange for documented losses.

You see, these tax deduction policies don't hurt the people in any way - they HELP the people. Politicians are angry that these tax deduction policies allow money to slip through their own hands and into the hands of the citizens! Politicians want to be able to dictate what happens with this money and how it was spent so they fight to eliminate policies that benefit both, companies and the citizens.

Other measures to "upstream" money (to move it around without being taxed for the movement of it) is to start your own separate LLC that offers "services" to your main, original LLC - "services" that receive a lower tax rate. In this way, by utilizing the benefits and privileges of corporations you can move your money to a lower tax bracket. Research Development, Marketing Services, Consulting Services, Sales agencies, Equipment leasing, and Real Estate are all examples of services that allow money to be "up streamed" and provide a tax deduction for your original LLC. Rich people know about all of these loopholes and have been utilizing them to avoid the government's "highway robbery".

Taxes are based on the profit that your company makes after expenses are paid. "Expenses" are the bills required to run your business, including paying your employees. If it costs you $10,000 a month to operate your business and you earn $15,000 a month in sales, then $5,000 is your profit - which must be taxed.

There are four types of expenses: Start-up expenses, Operating expenses, Inventory, and Capital expenses (loan payments). Some examples of business expenses that are tax deductible include, but are not limited to: office rent, business cards, incorporation fees, meals (50%), computers, phone bill, employees, auto allowance, travel, achievement awards, health insurance, dependant care, cafeteria plans, education /dues /subscriptions, retirement plans, and losses (historical).

Tax deductions are a major benefit to entrepreneurs which make it imperative to understand how to utilize them. The LLC provides numerous protective measures - if only we were taught all these things as children or in public schools.

A great benefit to prisoners who have organized their own LLC is that it can be ran by its owners OR- it can be "manager-managed" by a person or company who is not an owner of the LLC. If a prisoner decides to hire a manager to run the LLC (beneficial because they're out there in the free world) it's important to know this manager has a "fiduciary duty" to make decisions they believe are in the best interest of your company. It's a legal duty to make business decisions, spend the company's money and act in what they reasonably believe to be in the best interests of your LLC. They have a duty to act in good faith and with the utmost care.

This means that we can trust somebody to run our business while we're behind walls without worrying about shady business or someone trying to get over on us. This does not mean that the manager will always make the best business decisions, but it means they can't play us. One problem I've seen that most prisoners have while inside is not being able to trust anybody in the free world with their business (when not incorporated). People tend to believe that because we're in prison that we don't "need the money" -a justification to spend our money like it's their own. We bypass this problem by having a manager who has a fiduciary duty to be loyal to our LLC (ie. can't spend our money). Another bonus for the LLC!

Do you want the "list of owners" of your company to remain private? Do you (for whatever reason) want to keep it from the prison administration that you own/run a business? - An LLC can help you with that too! Not every state will keep the owner list private but each state provides different privileges to attract entrepreneurs to incorporate in their state. Wyoming is a state that does not list names of the owners of the LLC on the internet. The two best states to organize your LLC within are Wyoming and Nevada. Not only do they provide you all the benefits and protections of other states, Wyoming and Nevada have no state income tax or corporate tax! Organizing in these two states you won't be paying any state taxes on your profits. They do require an annual fee of $325 (Nevada) or $50 (Wyoming) but that's cheaper than paying state taxes. And, you don't even have to live in either of these states. If you don't reside there, all you have to do is pay a "Resident Agent" an annual fee (around $100) and you can organize in these states from any part of the country. The

Resident Agent has no part of your business and has nothing to do with it. They're just a required step to organize from out of state.

Additional benefits that Nevada and Wyoming provide those who organize in their states are:

• They protect "single member" LLCs (where most states require 2 or more owners)

• They don't share corporation information with the IRS

• They provide greater protections for officers and directors of the LLC

• They provide flexibility in management.

• They provide flexibility in capitalization and structuring

• AND, they provide privacy (only Resident Agent knows owner's information).

However, no protections ever apply to a criminal investigation. If any sketchy activity occurs, the veil will be pierced and will spill into the public eye. We're not educating ourselves to become better criminals; we're trying to become better citizens. Keep it legal-always.

Business note about the internet: one does not have to pay state tax for any business transactions done outside of the state you organized your LLC in. Always keep an eye open for any change in this law but this is good reason to run a business over the internet. You can easily make your own website via Shopify and have a business up and running overnight. Shopify charges you about $29 a month to run the page but it's customer friendly and easy to use. I had never even used a smart phone before but soon as I got my hands on a contraband cell phone in here, even I had a business up and running overnight via Shopify. It's that easy. And my bro did too - he began designing graphics and created his own clothing line, then had all of his clothes available for sale on his website within a week (utilizing a cell phone and Shopify). He's the one who inspired me to get my page up and running in the first place and to learn all about it. Bro was doing his thing!

The internet provides limitless opportunities these days. If you want your business to have any kind of success, you gotta have a presence on the internet. See the end of this chapter for a list of websites to choose from to help you build your storefront online.

As a prisoner, learn about the different kinds of corporate structures but focus specifically on the LLC. This is the structure that I guarantee you'll be using for any of your business endeavors. It's a beautiful structure. You can basically do whatever you want with it and shape it however you desire.

Take your education of this matter into your own hands. Learn more about LLCs, corporations, and business from the professionals. A great book to begin with is *"Start Your Own Corporation"* by Garrett Sutton (Rich Dad Advisor). Even though the title says "Corporation", the book focuses on LLC's and why they're a better choice for most entrepreneurs. But it does briefly discuss the history of corporations and summarizes the different structures.

The Small Business Administration (SBA) provides a list of steps that summarize what needs to be done to start your own business. From www.SBA.gov, 10 Steps to Starting your own Business:

1) Write a Winning Business Plan (provides tools and resources online)

2) Get Business Assistance and Training (free training and counseling services).

3) Choose a Business Location (comply with zoning laws)

4) Finance Your Business (government loans, venture capital, research grants)

5) Determine the Legal Structure of Your Business

6) Register a Business Name (learn which TIN from IRS)

7) Register for State and Local taxes (Obtain T.I.N.)

8) Obtain Business Licenses and Permits (federal, state, and local licenses)

9) Understand Employer Responsibilities

10) Find Local Assistance

You can save money by using "government surplus" items (commercial real estate, cars, furniture, computers, office equipment, etc.). Search their website to discover these deals. The Small Business Administration provides many resources to help your business get up and running. Don't ignore the assistance they provide, have your people look into it.

I'm a personal fan of author/attorney Garrett Sutton, author of the aforementioned book "Start Your Own Corporation". He's wrote several books to help entrepreneurs like us understand business techniques and get started today. Notice the first step to starting a business recommended by the SBA was to "Write a Winning Business Plan". This is a crucial step in any successful business and cannot be ignored, but most of us have no idea how to write a business plan. For this step, I suggest you read *"Writing Winning Business Plans"* by Garrett Sutton. This book lays out all the information required in an easy-to-read-and-understand language that will have you clearly expressing your business ideas on paper in no time. A business plan is not only used as a roadmap for you to follow as you go but is also the main factor in whether or not people will decide to invest in your business. The better your business plan is expressed on paper; the more likely people and banks will invest in your company - which leads us to step #4 being recommended by the SBA... Finance Your Business.

To get your business off the ground you're going to need financing. Anyone familiar with Rich Dad publications will recall OPM (Other People's Money). Smart entrepreneurs use OPM to fuel their business. Even rich people who don't need it are aware how easy it is to get others to invest in them. You don't need your own money to start a business... all you need is the idea. *Money follows the idea.* If you can express a good idea clearly within your business plan, investors will line up to give you money. Rich investors are always in search of new ways to force their money to make more money. They wanna see their money have babies (multiply) and the easiest way to do this is invest in a good idea. Investors receive either ownership rights to a small percentage or receive interest on their loan. OPM is available from avenues that you probably don't even know exist. At least I didn't know they existed until I read *"Finance Your Own Business"* by Garrett Sutton. This book is a mandatory read for anyone trying to utilize OPM to get your business started. See the end of this chapter for a list of internet resources used to finance your business.

But first, a quick summary of the types of loans designed for and available to people in our position.

• Microloans. Microloans are small, short-term loans offered through microlenders, which are nonprofit economic development organizations approved by the SBA. These loans are usually offered to neighborhood, mom-and-pop-type businesses, or those that have credit challenges. If you want to receive funds from microlenders, be prepared to fulfill their training and planning requirements (www.microbiz.org)

• SBA 7(a) loans. These loans are for distressed and underserved communities and are up to $250,000. This program targets communities such as minorities, women, veterans, and business in rural or low-income areas.

• CDFI's. Community Development Financial Institutions may provide funding for small businesses, microenterprises, nonprofit organizations, commercial real estate, and affordable housing. CDFI's are a crucial source of funding for small businesses that have been turned down for loans. They focus on low-income and/or minority communities, although they typically require collateral and/or personal guarantees.

• CDC/504 loan Programs. This loan is designed for business owners to purchase assets or finance real estate expansion, as well as nonprofit corporations that promote community economic development in specific geographic areas, usually underserved communities.

* Note about the SBA... they won't be the ones who actually give you a loan but they can guarantee 90% payment of the loan to the lender, which makes investors more likely to give you their money.

• Crowdfunding. This is when large amounts of people pool their money into a pot with the intent of investing in an entrepreneur.

These were just a few of the unheard-of loans that are available outside of your usual bank loans, credit unions, grants, and credit cards. Many more are available. If you believe in your business idea full heartedly, others will too.

"Your margin is my opportunity." - Jeff Bezos.

Judge your business idea by its ability to provide a solution to a problem with a potential market. Does your business help solve a problem you've discovered somewhere within the market? If so, explain how it solves this problem clearly enough and you'll have no problem at all financing your business.

Personal Traits of a Successful Entrepreneurs:

1) Vision

2) Courage

3) Creativity

4) Ability to withstand criticism

5) Ability to delay gratification

Some wise words of Garrett Sutton which have inspired me:

• *"Great business plans come from entrepreneurs willing to delay immediate gratification. They take risks and invest the time and energy necessary to gain relevant experience and education. They are not afraid of making mistakes or failing because mistakes and failures equal experience. They start small and build, recognizing experience leads to a greater ability. After paying the price, true entrepreneurs gain the knowledge to build a winning plan and winning business."*

• *"Successful businesses require great people first, great systems second, and great products third"*

• *"Your business plan is your roadmap to the future."*

• *"Your main goals should be measurable in time, dollars, quantity or comparison.... If you can't measure it, it's not a goal."*

• *"Sophisticated investors and lenders want to peek into your heart to see if you have what it takes to be successful. Their answer often lies in your Mission Statement. A company's mission is sacred to true entrepreneurs because it is the essence of who they are and why they are in business"*

This all may sound like hard work. I wouldn't necessarily label it as "hard" work but yes... it's a lot of work. If it wasn't, and if it was easy - everybody would do it. Your ability to work and your persistence is what will separate you from the masses and make you successful. Make work into a habit - a little bit of work every day grows exponentially into its own monster. You must be military minded with this shit, with everything you do. The Navy Seal's motto is "you have to earn your Trident every day." Great motto to live by. Especially in here, in prison. What else have we got to do with ourselves? Watch TV? — fuck that TV.

When planning for a business, you've got to be able to look into the future. You've got to have vision. "Thinking long term" is NOT natural for humans, it's a discipline we must develop. Discipline yourself. Keep the "Day 1" mentality in mind (the term used by Jeff Bezos) meaning that no matter how much success you've achieved, never get comfortable. Treat every day like it's the first day of business, grinding as hard as possible, treating it like it's "do or die". Amazon is a trillion-dollar business but Jeff

Bezos is not complacent. His success has inspired him to work even harder, even smarter, and he's revolutionizing the world.

Never let somebody kill your vision. There's always going to be haters out there and people praying on your downfall. Feed from their negative energy. Bezos said, "Look in the mirror and ask if you agree with critics. If not, water the garden and ignore the weeds."

You got this! It's on you to make it happen.

Once you've developed your business idea and have some form of product or service to sell, the next step is to market and advertise whatever it is that you offer. This is the most important step in becoming successful because in order to make a sale people have to know that you have something to sell. The more people who know, the better. You've gotta get your business out there in front of the public eye. It's the only way to really make it happen and is what differentiates your hustle from everyone else's. Here is a list of marketing weapons, all of which must be used to push your product or services. There's no reason to neglect any of these weapons.

- Name (of target product and company)
- Niche (group of targeted customers)
- Quality
- Color
- Logo
- Theme
- Distribution
- Pricing
- Customer Email list
- Business cards
- Stationary
- Inserts
- Contests and Sweepstakes
- Roadside Stands
- Gift Baskets
- Attire
- Music
- Neatness
- Smiles
- Publicity Contacts.
- Brand-name Awareness
- Reputation
- Paid Advertisements
- Newspaper Ads
- Magazine Ads
- Radio Commercials
- TV Commercials
- Outdoor Billboards
- Social Media Influencers
- Models
- YouTube Promotional Videos
- Online Ads
- Pen Pal sites
- Blogs and Podcasts
- Community Involvement
- Take-One Boxes
- Window Displays
- Circulars
- Books and Articles
- Gift Certificates
- Testimonials
- Tie-ins with others.
- Newsletters
- Posters
- Bumper Stickers

- Banners
- Inside Signs
- Blimps
- Consultations
- Demonstrations
- Direct Mail Postcards
- Postcard Decks
- Mall Booth
- Door Hangers
- Bookmarks
- Outside Signs
- Word-of-mouth
- Brochures
- Public Relations
- Website and/or App
- Catalogs
- Credibility
- Satisfied Customers

Practice all of these marketing weapons and you are guaranteed to have a successful business. Remember that you are the face of your brand. When people respect you, they'll respect your business and personal integrity will reflect the integrity of your business. Carry your product around with you or speak about your services. If you wrote a book, bring a copy of your book with you everywhere that you go. Send a copy to your friends in other prisons. Circulate your work. If your service is doing legal work, carry your binder or manilla envelope everywhere; always have a pen on you - no matter what. *A gentleman always has a pen.*

When you get your business up and running, or are looking to network, hit me up! Maybe we can co-op on a project! Maybe we can help each other advertise our products within our personal circles and environments.

<u>SYO Business Resources</u>

www.sba.gov (government surplus items, assistance, loan approval)

ww.irs.gov (tax information, EIN, TIN, etc.)

<u>Set fees to incorporate for you:</u>

www.corporatedirect.com

www.legalzoom.com

<u>Lending and Loans:</u>

www.acoworks.org

www.microbiz.org

www.ofn.org/cdfi-locator

www.ncua.org

www.grameenamerica.org

www.kiva.org

www.lendingclub.com

www.kickstarter.com

www.prosper.com

www.indiegogo.com

www.fastweb.com

www.peoplefundit.com

www.rockethub.com

www.smallenot.com

Find Lost Money:

www.unclaimedproperty.com

www.missingmoney.com

See Credit Scores:

www.annualcreditreport.com

www.credit.com

Establish Business Credit:

www.uline.com

www.businesscreditsuccess.com

www.self.com

www.salary.com (helps you figure good salary numbers).

www.listyourself.net (list your business cell phone online)

www.gimp.com (put together your image and font)

Researching Niches:

www.google.com/trends

www.pickfu.com

www.Surveymonkey.com

Domain Name Registrations:

www.namesilo.com

www.godaddy.com

www.namecheap.com

www.porkbun.com (author's choice)

www.geni.us/ (allows you to create a domain name with or without a website and attach Amazon's "affiliate link" with the domain name. They will forward you directly to Amazon if someone types in the domain name, which you then receive 4-6% affiliate commission from any purchases made).

Storefront Website Design Pages:

www.shopify.com.

www.woocommerce.com

www.bigcommerce.com

www.bigcartel.com

www.godaddy.com/airo

Website Design Pages without Storefront readily available:

www.squarespace.com

www.wix.com

www.weebly.com

<u>Free and Paid classes:</u>

www.coursera.com

www.futurelearn.com

www.lynda.com

www.udemy.com

www.designschool.canva.com

<u>Fonts and Images:</u>

www.1001 fonts.com

www.dafont.com

www.fonts.google.com

www.images.google.com

www.dreamstime.com

www.shutterstock.com

<u>Print-On-Demand (POD) websites:</u>

www.theprintful.com

www.printify.com

www.cafepress.com

www.society6.com

www.zazzle.com

How to receive your business' EIN? www.irs.gov

Apply for an EIN with the IRS assistance tool. It will guide you through questions and ask for your name, social security number, address, and your "doing business as" (DBA). Your nine-digit federal tax ID becomes available immediately upon verification.

Some Business Ideas

We've discussed "how" to start your own business but you may now be asking yourself "what" kind of business could you actually start from behind bars. There's a lot of different things you could do depending on your abilities, your creativity, and your network team. When contemplating what type of business you'd like to begin, it's best to start with the economic principle of "supply and demand". The "demand" is any need or want that is missing from the market place, a hole for you to fill; whereas "supply" is how much of this product/service is available to match the need/want, the demand.

"Supply and demand" is really an equation that 1) tells you what the market place is either missing or has too much of; and 2) balances out products/services. If there is a demand for a product and you supply it - you will make money. If the supply is low but the demand is high, the prices go up. If the supply is plentiful, the prices will balance out by dropping to a reasonable price. But if the demand (want/need) for the supply is low, prices drop dramatically. There's no value in a product nobody wants.

Supply = the product/service, and the amount of it available

Demand = the want or need of the product/service, the desire for it

"Supply and demand" is an essential economic principle you should understand before ever venturing into business.

From in prison, we have an entirely different aspect we must face and include into the principle of supply and demand. We have to be realistic with ourselves when determining what we can actually do from in here, what demands we can actually supply. Out there, we could figure out a method to supply any demand but from in here the task becomes a little bit more tricky. Our options are limited and we have to depend on people from the outside world to assist us. That dependency makes us, as well as our dreams, feel like a burden to our loved ones. We must practice divine patience with this matter, understand we're working on other people's terms, operating on other people's time. That's not easy for an ambitious person like me and I'm sure you know exactly what I'm talking about. It's just a fact of our life that we have to accept; being incarcerated forces you to become dependent. Being dependent on others has a way of humbling that ego, although I still dislike it.

However, lets assume you have a networking team out there, a few people who will move and groove for you...as that's half the battle right there. But now what? What kind of opportunities are available, and realistic, for someone incarcerated? As iron sharpens iron, I've decided to share a few of my business ideas and goals with you. I'd like to achieve all of these goals but, whether I do or don't, I have zero qualms with he who accomplishes the task first or who does it better than me. I'd like to uplift us as a people which begins by sharing ideas with each other. And as Drake said, "It aint about who did it first, it's about who did it right." You've got the innovators, but most times it's the imitators who profit from an idea. The market rewards whoever provides the best services and products. *"If a man can write a better book, preach a better sermon, or make a better mouse trap than his neighbor, though he builds his house in the woods, the world will make a path to his door."* - Ralph Waldo Emerson

Go and get those rewards! Make the world come to you. And, if you have any business ideas or opportunities you'd like to share with me, maybe we can partner up and make something happen. Manifest some dreams into realities. That's what life's about, right? Well... lets get to it.

As you can see, a "publishing company" was an idea I've decided and been able to act upon. For me, as a writer, it only made sense... but I went into it well aware of the dedication, determination, persistence, and years of work it'd take to make it make cents, and eventually dollars. It's 2024 now and I've been working to get this ball rolling since 2017... and how many different lives I feel I've lived since then, so many different chapters experienced, ups and downs, heartbreaks and emotional rollercoasters. So much has happened but I remained myself. I kept pushing, stayed focused, and you've finally heard about Best Self Publications. McDonalds figured out a system and shared it with the world; Best Self Publications figured out a system and shared it with prisoners. However, we're not a monopoly... if you'd like to start your own publishing company it's relatively simple - and cheap. In fact, I've explained exactly how I do it, step-by-step, in my upcoming book "How to Self-Publish from a Prison cell for Under $100". It's about how to publish your book but includes how to turn this experience into a publishing company, blueprint included. Recommended read for anyone interested in publishing.

Another company that I was a step away from operating was a "vendor company", my own catalog for prisoners that fulfilled a demand I saw missing from all other vendors/catalog companies. My catalog was advertising products being sold through Amazon, with the goal of providing people who have limited internet access the opportunity to utilize the services offered by the Amazon market. My catalog was going to be a "reverse e-commerce" business, meaning that we had no actual products to sell (which lowered our risk). We were to be a "service" that advertised items currently being sold at Amazon (as well as my publishing company's services). With a Prime membership there is no shipping/handling fee so we were going to advertise books, calendars, jewelry, religious items, etc. for the same price that Amazon charges but tax our customers a shipping/handling fee, creating our margin for profit. There would be no interference between customer and Amazon; we'd purchase the order and have Amazon ship it directly to the customer. My people could do all this from a laptop, never having to leave home or meet anybody. The initial investment was the cost of producing catalogs. I thought it was genius, and it still is, but all crashed and burned to hell right after I invested a couple thousand dollars into it. Right after organizing my LLC and getting the ball rolling came the vicissitudes of life. My prison released a memo stating that, effective immediately, inmates were no longer authorized to utilize any book vendor besides Edward R. Hamilton's Bargain Books. I was devastated after reading that memo. Not only were my business goals affected but my entire life revolved around educating myself through reading... and no longer was Amazon's book selection available to me. My soul took a hit that day. A month prior to that I had just lost my state-court level appeal and things were looking gloom. Then, my girlfriend at the time (who owned a large portion of the LLC) ghosted me without an explanation. Good times!

These aren't excuses to quit or give up, and I still have not, but I did let that LLC go to waste... as well as a couple thousand dollars. The universe showing me that I wasn't ready for that business venture at the time. I was acting upon an under developed idea... a sin within business. And I paid the price for this lesson. However, a vendor/catalog company is still an excellent idea. The demand is there for a better all-around service, someone just needs to fill the gap (and become rich doing so).

Ever had a dream of starting your own "clothing/accessory line"? It's relatively simple. If you recall from the previous chapter, my friend started his own brand of clothing from a cell phone we had and set up an entire business that required no physical human presence. The advancement of technology with the evolution of the internet has brought opportunities to inmates (and the rest of society) that haven't always been available at the click of a button. But now they are! There are several Print-On-Demand companies that deal with clothing and any other accessory you can think of. Apps like Printify and Printful (see resources in the appendix) allow you to upload images you've designed and print them on clothing or other accessories of choice. Being a Print-On-Demand company (keyword being "demand") these items are saved into the site exactly how you designed them and are only printed whenever someone makes a purchase. Whenever there is a demand (a purchase), the company supplies the product. No products are printed before being purchased.

Make your own website (see resources) then link your POD account to your website (easily done). This allows for you to advertise your products to the world, to make a name for your brand. Whenever someone purchases an item from your website, the order is automatically processed through your POD account, who then ships the product to the customer. The profit is deposited directly into your bank account and you never even saw the product. All you did was click a few buttons on your cell phone or laptop, and watched magic happen. It's so simple that an inmate with a cell phone can do it!

If you do a really good job at developing your brand name and the sale of your t-shirts catch momentum, you can apply to be advertised on Amazon through Amazon Merch. I say "apply" because Amazon doesn't accept everybody's clothing brand. If they did, their marketplace would be diluted with bullshit clothes. Getting your t-shirts accepted into Amazon Merch should be a goal for your clothing brand (if you specialize in t-shirts) because your sales increase dramatically. Amazon is aware of these gains you'll receive which is a reason not everybody's shirts make it to their marketplace.

However, outside of your personal clothing line, Amazon's marketplace is available to entrepreneurs and small business owners who sell other products. Here comes the now popular "drop shipping" that most entrepreneurs have at least heard about, if not indulged within. What is drop shipping? It's purchasing products from "point A", having them shipped to an online market place of "point B", sold there, and you collect the profit off the top. Again, this is all done without ever seeing or touching the product.

Here's the most simple and popular method of drop shipping:

Step One: Choose a Top 100 selling product on Amazon.

Step Two: Find manufacturers in China via Alibaba.com (China's version of Amazon, except mass productions of items)

Step Three: Have the manufacturer ship the products to Amazon's FBA (Fulfillment By Amazon) warehouse

Step Four: Once the bird has landed at the warehouse, Amazon lets you sell it under your own brand name to consumers.

Step Five: Collect the profit!... and do it again.

Alibaba is one of the world's largest companies. You can find a manufacturer for almost anything you can imagine. Amazon's FBA services cost approximately $400/year (or $25/month) - a reasonable price for what this service provides your company. They package and ship your product directly to the consumer, depositing the profit directly into your bank account. They even warehouse your products for you until they are sold.

If you don't want to deal with Alibaba and are searching for products closer to home, you can even purchase Amazon Pallets from a local warehouse. Amazon sells pallets of returned items for a discounted rate - even though there's nothing wrong with the products. You must purchase the entire pallet as a whole with whatever items come inside of it but you're receiving a deal. You can sell each of these items right back through Amazon or Ebay or Facebook Marketplace... for fair market value. This hustle will require someone on the streets to assist you but, again... profit. It's an easy flip. Many companies sell pallets at discounted rates, for whatever reason. You just have to search for them.

With a wholesale license, many companies (such as Nike) will sell products at a discounted rate so that you can sell them at retail price, making nice profits.

Get your wholesale license and most distributors open their doors to you, offering major discounts and leaving plenty of room for you to come up legally.

Are you an artist? Are you creative? Or, are you around people who will sell you some artwork? I've also thought about starting up a "greeting card company" using pictures drawn up by guys in here. Companies like Vistaprint will let you upload the pictures and mass produce greeting cards that you can sell for profit. Why sell hundreds of different drawings when you can mass produce a few pictures on greeting cards or T shirts or even phone cases? An artist may be able to sell a drawing... but then what? To make any more money they have to spend time and energy drawing a new one. That's cool... especially if art is your hobby you use to pass time and get by... but an entrepreneur will try to capitalize as much as possible from each piece of art. Greeting cards are a simple way to make money over and over from the same pictures without having to expend additional labor.

Even if you don't have any artists around you who you can profit from their drawings, these days apps can instantly generate pictures of ideas. ChatGPT app is a magical device to keep in your toolbox, as well as Claude. Both are artificial intelligence but can make the goals of an inmate much more simple to accomplish. The cover of this book was generated by an app like this. All I did was type in "The Prisoner Manifesto", asking it to generate an image, and out came my book cover. Because I'm unaware of the copyright protections of these images, your safest bet is to have a graphic designer alter the image by at least 30% before using it to make any profits.

ChatGPT and Claude are new to me. There is so much more I'd like to learn about what it's capable of creating. For example, I'd like to see what it will do if I upload a "black and white" drawing, then ask it to graphic design the image with color and sharpness... and make it look better! Who knows, but I do know that a greeting card company will turn some profit. Especially if you're creative enough. Search Fiverr for any assistance you may need... for pretty much anything.

While still on the topic of artwork, another idea I have would be a magazine subscription or book of artwork pulled from the public domain, compiled with different fonts/texts, as well as inmate's artwork. There's a demand for a useful book of artwork that is better than the generic versions we've all seen.

How about a "TV Guide subscription"... a list of all the channels that inmates actually watch so that we don't need two or three different subscriptions just to cover all of our channels? What prisoner wouldn't want to subscribe to that?

Got something to say but don't really enjoy writing? Start your own inmate podcast. There are plenty of apps that record both ends of people's phone calls so it would be relatively simple to produce a podcast from in here...especially if your prison provides ample phone time each day.

Ever getting out of prison? Record your life and your transition back into society, all the struggles and hardships that go along with it, and your first -year out there with us as a "documentary". People would eat that up like candy... especially if you did a good job producing it and overcame your struggles, coming out a hero at the end.

These were just a few ideas I've had over the years that I'm sure many of us have shared at some point. Each of us have different passions and will chase different dreams and goals. Right now, my true self is telling me to pursue a writing career so I'm following wherever my passions lead me. If you learn about one of these ideas from my book and decide to manifest it, let me know! It'd bring joy to my day to know my words have affected you in some way. Again, if you wanna collaborate, hit me up! If you start a podcast, send me an invite. I've got some shit to say that could

stir up the status quo.

What If" by Becky Hemsley

What if the mermaids are all of the women

Cast overboard 'cause of old superstition

Drowning beneath the waves, gasping

Then forging a tail with the strength they have left?

And what if the dragons, with their breath ablaze

Were once little lizards all thrown to the flames

choking on smoke and then swallowing flares.

Then rising up, claiming that power as theirs?

And maybe the vampires favour the night

Cause they've been kept in the dark most of their lives.

Starved of companions, affection and love

"Til they have no choice but to feed on our blood.

Yes, what if these creatures of magic and myth

Are those who've known darkness but chosen to live

Chosen to breath and to rise and survive

To harness adversity, hoping they'll thrive?

And what if you too have been thrown to the waves,

Befriended the night and encountered the flames.

And so you've assumed that you're destined to burn,

To drown in the darkness-

But what if you learned...

That maybe your story is not over yet

That there are still pages that need to be read

Pages of oceans that you're yet to swim,

Fiery chapters for you to breathe in.

Lines built on words that are so full of light

of such warmth and strength, they inspire you to write.

And what if you choose now to pick up a pen

And write through the night til you came to the end?

And what if you read it back?

Well, then you'll find

That your story has always held magic inside.

Writing and Self-Publishing

The most important tool of expression that an inmate has at his disposal is writing. Writing down thoughts and ideas, sharing them with the world, is an activity that all inmates should participate in. It doesn't matter if you're a great writer or not. Nobody was born an author or a journalist. Like all things, with practice comes skill. Writing is the strongest weapon in our arsenal but so many of us fail to ever pick up a pen. *Many people don't even own a pen!*

Everything going on inside your head will always remain inside your head if you don't pick up a pen and share it with somebody or put it down on paper for the future generations to read and learn about who you really are. In here, not too many people care to sit there and listen to your complaints or hear about your past because... we're all going through the same thing. I already understand that the lunch tray was trash so I don't need to hear you telling me about it. Eat it and move on.

We all have a desire to express ourselves but most of us are too lazy to do it in a way that makes somebody else actually care to listen. If you've been in prison for any substantial amount of time, you'll understand how tiring it is to hear people talk about the exact same thing over and over again, year after year. But I understand we only go through this repetitive process because we are struggling inside and we want something to change. I get it, I really do – but complaining to each other about it isn't going to make anything change.

The pen is the sword of today. Was anybody born being able to use a sword? No. They practiced over and over because their livelihoods depended on it. Same thing with us today and our pens. A few years back, a new maximum-security housing unit was opened at the facility I was housed at and I was in the group of first inmates to be placed in it. The living conditions were unbearable and the pain of our struggles was being heard from the lips of all of us who lived there. We didn't know what to do. Were we just gonna let them do it to us? Were we just gonna sit there and suffer until they broke half of us? Not many people are built to last through this kind of oppression, many lack resiliency and fortitude. But there had to be a way for us to fight our living conditions without our environment exploding into violence (this unit had been built as the result of a deadly riot that had just occurred). We had been voicing our problems to the unit staff but they are only peons who have no power over our living conditions. They couldn't change things if they wanted to, they're paid to follow the administration's orders... not change things.

Our voices could travel no further than the ears of the unit staff who were trapped there with us and already overwhelmed by their jobs. Necessity caused me to discover the petition process. The petition process showed me the power of a pen. I sat down and organized different petitions, then had my fellow inmates read and sign them, in solidarity. I could see hope light up in their eyes for the first time since being housed there as they read over my words. Staff even tried to stop us from circulating our petitions but they couldn't because we have the right to do so. Through writing we were able to accomplish something that 62 verbal voices failed to do without a pen. We ended up winning 8 out of the 16 petitions we filed, which was a big victory for us because many rules were changed and conditions became more endurable.

Words can travel outside of our housing units when we write them down, can last into the future if we'd like them to. Words can be crafted to portray thoughts, feelings and emotions, struggles, and ideas that nobody outside of prison is aware exist. Writing is a form of art, a craft that all of us should practice OR at least know how to practice when necessity arises.

A pen has the power of altering the future when the right mind beholds it. You are that right mind! I look at my pen like it's a magical wand, a few flicks can change the universe if I know the right spells. *Spell out a spell, curse 'em in cursive. Replace the pistol with a pen... always keep it on you because you never know when you might need it.*

As an inmate, the pen is our voice. It's the means by which we can be heard outside of these walls, by which our thoughts can travel into the minds of millions of people.

There's so many different things we can write about. Ideas are limitless. I pick up new ideas every day that are inspired from hearing people speak. Ideas are everywhere. Creativity is a synthesis of information you've acquired. Absorb everything and see your mind as a synthesizer.

There's so much change that can be made if we apply ourselves to the craft of writing. One thing that we can all agree on is that we need social change and prison reformation, but how will society know of our problems if we don't get it out there so they can become aware? They won't. We've got a momentum right now, there's a small current of energy beginning to favor the idea of prison reform. Let's add life to it! People are starting to watch, people are starting to feel, and citizens have came together to fight... but who's trying to continue fighting for somebody who won't fight for themselves? We don't go for that in here so why would they go for that out there? You already know what happens to the inmate who refuses to physically fight for himself in here so why would we not apply that same mentality to the bigger picture? Why do we think people in the world see it any differently when they're fighting for us? If they look inside and see that we're not even fighting for ourselves, they're gonna begin to think that we're not worth fighting for. We can't allow that to happen.

Society can't hear our cries, the pain of our struggle, because our oppressors have divided us and because we don't write! The time is now for us to come together in mind, through power of pen, to break down the walls of confinement! Apply yourself to the craft of writing, every day. It's by writing every day that one becomes a writer.

Write for a minimum of 30 minutes each day and eventually it will become a habit. These writings add up over time and eventually you've compiled an entire book! One page of writing every day for a year is 365 pages... that's damn near two books! Maybe three, and how many years do you have to serve? Just think about it. A little something positive every day compounds over time into something much bigger. The sum of the whole is greater than all of its parts. Spend some time writing, every day, just like you do your exercise routine. This *isn't* some "risk worth taking", *this is a mathematical fact*. It's a mandatory act that we need to perform each day if we truly care about ourselves, our freedom, our future. Talk is cheap, but writing has value. There's nothing to lose and everything to gain.

"Is the pen mightier than a sword? Can words have so much power? Consider the Bible, the Koran, Das Kapital, The Wealth of Nations. Only words, and yet they have moved nations and destroyed empires. Words are powerful beasts, and the ability to control them makes the writer a potent foe. If you are a writer, you are a dangerous entity. If you are a good writer, you are a positive menace." – Unknown

Stephen King said *"If you want to be a writer, you must do two things above all else; read a lot and write a lot. There's no way around these two things that I'm aware of, no short cut"*. Lucky for us, we have nothing but time to read and write. We have no real societal distractions that take up our days or our focus. We're being housed in a warehouse with nothing else to do - a TV being given to us in the way we give a pacifier to a baby. "Here, take this and shut up." I have to say this in my writings because I say it everywhere else in my regular life - Fuck that TV. Anyone who knows me will tell you that I live by that... I do not fuck with that TV, which I call "the box" or "the devil". It's a distraction-used to fill our minds with bullshit and weaken our resiliency. It's used to sedate us. I don't use drugs to escape my reality, I don't use the TV to escape my reality either. *Reality is something we must embrace in order to change it, and we can't change something we constantly run from.* In my head, TV is simply another drug, pumping lies into our brain and feeding us nonsense. Federal prisons don't even allow prisoners to have TVs in their cell, I think state prisoners should choose to live like that. Discipline yourself.

Don't get me wrong... I'm not advising you to never watch TV or avoid it like the plague. I'm suggesting you limit yourself, only watch it for a specific amount of time and avoid "mind numbing" shows. Don't be dependent on it for your sanity (or insanity, however you choose to view what "sane" entails). You can't grow if you read or write for 3 minutes a day but watch TV for 3 hours a day. It's common sense. Read for two hours a day, write for an hour a day, exercise for an hour or two each day, and watch TV for no more than an hour a day - and see how drastically your life will change, how much sharper your mind and body become. Witness how much better you feel inside mentally, physically, emotionally, and spiritually. Purify yourself from the evils of television. And remember: they only give it to us to sedate us, to pacify us, to make their own jobs as babysitters, as cattle farmers, as simple as possible. They don't allow us to purchase it out of the goodness of their heart or because they care or for our pleasure. It's a weapon they use against us in the battle for our minds. You know it and I know it. Go tell 3 people today "Fuck that TV!" (spread the word). I could go on and on about how much I dislike it and my reasons why, I could take you down the rabbit hole with me, but I may just keep that as the subject for another book entirely. The purpose behind this chapter is to express how valuable our time is, how we shouldn't waste it, and how writing can be the means by which we are freed from oppression.

We live in an era when anybody can publish a book, basically with a few clicks of a button. In the same way that musical artists now have the means to be independent of a label via social media platforms and streaming services, the internet has granted writers the freedom to get our books in print without the need of a publisher to accept our work. There are now multiple platforms that offer a service called Print-On-Demand (POD). This service provides us the ability to upload our writings to a platform, which will then advertise our books through its website or vendor catalogs before ever printing or manufacturing a copy.

Through a POD service, the book is not actually materialized until somebody makes a purchase of your book. Soon as a copy is purchased, the POD service prints one copy of your book and ships it to the buyer. Until a purchase is made, no physical copy of your book is available - but it's available for purchase via the website.

These services have been a game changer, especially for the inmate population, and the benefits are endless. We can now serve the public with any/all of our writings and there is no "go between middle man" who decides whether our writings are worthy of the market or not. The market itself now decides our work's worth (as well as the amount of hustle we each have as businessmen) but one thing for sure is that the market is now open to us. How YouTube and TikTok have been platforms for musical artists to upload their amateur videos and market themselves, POD services play that role for us as inmates who can now upload our writings and market ourselves.

For me personally, it's not about the money... my ultimate goal is social justice and prison reform... but I won't complain about adding a few pennies to my pocket, as neither should you. You deserve to be paid for your work but that profit has got to go back into our fight for freedom. I maintain that freedom is the ultimate goal of every prisoner. If that's the goal then why waste money on anything that doesn't push us closer to that goal?

The door to the market has been kicked down through POD services but we're the ones who have to take the steps to walk through it. Nobody is gonna do it for us. Success or failure is upon our own shoulders; you're responsible for the decisions you make today. Allow no excuses to justify your contrary actions. Freedom is the goal, lets get to it.

How many POD services are available and what do they each offer? I'm personally a fan of everything Amazon - Jeff Bezos is a hero to me, a living genius within our time who will be remembered thousands of years from now, so I choose to deal with Amazon's KDP Service. KDP is one of the fastest (and free) ways to help writers publish their books in Amazon's bookstore. It requires no upfront charges and will pay for the cost of printing/shipping using the money from a customer's purchase of your book. Yes, KDP collects a fee for this service (as it should) but you can still earn up to 40% royalties (profit), minus the cost of the book, from the sale of each of your books. Remember, Amazon has provided the KDP service for you to publish your works and has placed your writings within the world's biggest bookstore (making it simple for anyone to find and purchase your work). This is well worth the fee they collect from each sale.

As a rule of thumb, charge under $10 for any work below 50,000 words and above $10 for anything above 50,000 words. But hey, this just a suggestion. You're the boss of this company - if you can sell a 40,000 word book for $50, absolutely go for it! Just be realistic with yourself and your hustle.

Another POD service is Create Space. Through Create Space your works will ultimately end up in Amazon's Bookstore, as well as be made available to some libraries and their own e-stores. Create Space helps you get up to 70% of your royalties from book sales but they make you use a Create Space ISBN # to get access to their libraries and academic institutions. What this means is that Create Space will always have rights over your works (whereas Amazon does not). This service is a great place to get started if you want to be able publish a work just to get it out to family and people in your community.

The last POD service I'll mention is Ingram Spark. They make getting your work to readers relatively easy and your books will be available to purchase through Barnes and Noble.

Each service has their own pros and cons that you should look into but, as with everything, I recommend Amazon's KDP. One of my favorite benefits this service offers is the Amazon Author Profile. I find this to be a major benefit to inmates who wish to be taken seriously. As soon as you have at least one book on Amazon, the author profile is available to you and the world. It's free and allows you to upload your author picture and bio, some additional pictures, some videos, some book reviews, blurbs, as well as links to your website, social media, and blog pages. I'd suggest that you even include your prison address in your bio as a way for potential pen pals and fans to contact you! Just think about it, this is Amazon we're talking about here.... the world's biggest market place... and they're allowing us to be participants. Take advantage of this opportunity.

One last note on POD services.... having on-demand printing means that your work will never be out of stock and will never go out of print. Time spent wisely could produce an entire list of works that you leave behind for posterity or used to change the world while you're still in it. Whatever you wanna do.

I like to use the term "works" rather than the term "books" because there are many more forms of writing than the term "books" clearly identifies. Here's a list of publication ideas other than actual books:

• Reports - you can write a report about a general topic of knowledge or any interesting events you know of. These can be sold or printed on computer pages. You can also reprint or rewrite other people's reports to add to your list of knowledge you have available for sale.

• Booklets - if you just want to write - something short (typically 20,000 words or less), you can write and publish a booklet about anything. I've seen people use booklets as a way to clear up rumors or propaganda that has been falsely spread about somebody, writing and publishing the proof and the story on Amazon - and people bought it up. Almost like a form of local gossip news. Later, you can make your booklets as part of a larger book, or write booklets as a means to advertise your larger book. Booklets can also be used as a Pocket Book Edition to a larger book. Use your imagination.

• Short Stories and Articles - these publications can be used to get your name out there as an author or business man, and are typically defined as being under 10,000 words. They can be published in magazines that will even pay you for them. Probably pocket change, but you're still being paid for your time.

• Novellas - basically the same thing as a short story, just a little longer. A novella is over 10,000 words but under 50,000.

• Online Publications- topics are specific, pertaining to the website but are easy to be published because space is unlimited online.

• Blogs - short writings about whatever you want that you can publish on your personal blog page. Blogs can later be published within a larger work. See facebook.com/freenicholas

• Newsletters - self-explanatory. Can be used by you and other fellow inmates to spread your ideas, lives, and goals amongst other prisoners across other states and other joints.

• E-shorts/E-books- all of the above but sold digitally. They can help spread your name and your work.

• Comics - a mix of words and pictures to create a novel.

• Children's books - basically a poem, broken down by placing one line on each page along with some amateur artwork. You'd be surprised how successful and popular children's books are.

•Movie Scripts - a list of dialogue between characters and explaining what the scene should be, serves to film a movie or guide a play.

• Poetry - can be used as music lyrics, sold as a ghost writer, or published within a book as compilations. Also can be sold as the inside of greeting cards.

Before moving on from why all prisoners need to write, I want to share some game about self-publishing and writing that I've picked up from other authors over the years.

I've got to give a shout out to Mike Enemigo, an author serving a sentence of life imprisonment but is still publishing books from behind the walls. His marketing skills allowed for his book *Jailhouse Publishing* to make its way into my hands while I was serving 13 months in solitary confinement after being caught with a cell phone (you know how it goes). I dissected his book and I can honestly say that it changed my life. It inspired me, for starters, but it also shared many keys to have a successful career publishing books from behind bars. Here's some of the game I picked up from his book but I highly recommend that you buy yourself a personal copy. It's worth the investment.

- Reporting from behind the wall matters. History is shaped by those who record it
- The art of writing consists in the arrangement of words
- Collect information and ideas for the book you want to write and keep it inside a manilla envelope.
- Many prisoners write books but the key to success is the execution of getting those books to the market. *Execution is key!*

• Building a writing and publishing career is a building process. Very few writers hit a home run on their first book. Reason being, they don't have the experience they need to hit the home run.

• Simplify, and concentrate your forces. Do not overcomplicate the process.

• At the end of everything you write, give a 3-4 sentence bio and point readers back to your author platform.

• Making a six-figure living as a writer or journalist is not about strategy; it's about mindset, lifestyle, and habit.

• Profitable writers write everyday, whether the mood hits them or not.

• While you're locked up, pump out as many books as you can.

• Target new audiences like Canada, UK, Germany, etc. and/or make audio books for the new generation.

• *Not everyone can see your vision, so you have to believe in yourself enough to stay committed.*

In Mike Enemigo's own words, *"before, I put a lot of effort and drive into negative things - thuggin', basically. So the things I did to get the bag was, essentially, just getting me further into debt, you feel me? I knew I had to transform my hustle if I wanted to truly be successful, and this writing thing is a major part of that .... So, I went from dope dealer to hope dealer. I dreamed of slangin' birds, but now I'm achieving my dreams slangin' words, you feel me? I'm shipping boxes of books like I wanted to ship bricks. And not only am I completely legit, I'm making more money now than I ever did with my grimy endeavors."*

Who of us can't feel that? I know we all desire to transform our hustle, to be legit and never have to worry about these people fuckin' with us ever again. I don't know if Mike meant it how I understood it to mean, or maybe I just felt it like this because I was struggling in the hole at the time, but the "debt that chasing the bag puts us in" is, essentially, the punishment that comes because of it. Time is all of our most valuable resource, and from this perspective I asked myself "is 13 months in the hole worth the bag that I was trying to chase, especially when throughout that time I lost all the money I'd earned, as well as all the relationships I had developed? Is the irreparable damage being caused to my psyche worth the reward?" And this punishment is what I began to see as the "debt" that comes from the game. Or, from a street perspective, is a million dollars from hustling worth the twenty-year prison sentence you'll eventually receive? Absolutely not. No amount of money is as valuable as our time or our freedom. We need to bring back to our conscious (and keep it there) how valuable freedom really is to us. *Give me liberty or give me death...* NOT give me some money and then make me pay for it with twenty-years imprisonment. It just doesn't make sense any more once we realize there are different opportunities available to those who choose to educate themselves and utilize it.

Mike goes on to say, *"Stay positive and motivated. When you live inside a box, you must learn to think outside of one. Be creative. Confinement can cause a man to tap into the deepest parts of the mind. Take advantage of that, be dedicated and determined, and you'll be surprised at what you can pull off. This is my proof. My story is a testament that you must never give up. Your first idea is rarely your best one, and the road to success is not a straight shot."*

I appreciate your work, Mike. Keep pushing that pack.

Another highly recommended book for prison writers is called *The Sentences That Create Us: Crafting a Writers Life in Prison* edited by Caits Meissner, a PEN America book. Beautiful title for prison writers, isn't it? This is another mandatory read for anyone who wants to take this craft seriously. They've taken prison writing to a higher level. And, PEN America gives this book away <u>for free</u> to any inmate who requests a copy. This book is worth the investment of time! Here's a few gems I picked from it:

• Publication doesn't make you a writer, writing does.

• Every writer is an avid reader of thought-provoking books.

• If you won't be the conscience of your world, there won't be one. If you don't tell the tale, no one will be left to do so.

- There's no such thing as "writer's block", which is simply fear of writing badly, masquerading as something that sounds official. Every writer writes badly everyday- it's how you get to the center of things.

- It's more important to prioritize reliability over raw talent, because of prison's volatility

- Remember: write while you research, be relentless in your pursuit of allies, always keep your word, show benefit to the community, prioritize reliability in collaborators, be transparent, seek honest feedback, be diligent and patient.

- Always ask yourself "What's the intention of your writing?" Always remember our primary goal.

- Words are the ingredients of expression. Learn how to engage the reader.

- Write with the heart first, then all else will follow.

On Collaborating through the Walls:

- Respect the boundaries

- Take chances on unlikely new relationships

- Cultivate divine patience

- Share opportunities with others inside

- Believe deeply in the worth of your own gifts

- Keep learning and growing

Writing and Editing Guidelines:

• Guard against redundancy and repetition

• Be ruthless in the pursuit of descriptive and emotional clarity

• Eliminate useless words

• Vary your sentences

• Always and without fail, read your work aloud

Types of words:

• Noun - a concept, object, person, or animal

• Pronoun- a word that stands in for a noun

• Adjective - a word the describes or modifies a noun

• Article- a word that shows whether a noun is indefinite/unspecific or definite/specific

• Verb-an action

• Adverb - a word that modifies a verb or adjective

• Conjunction- words that connect other words of sentences (and, but, or)

• Preposition-words that link to nouns and often describe a relationship

• Interjection - something that a person exclaims, like hey!

The Sentences That Create Us is so much more than I have expressed and there's an abundance of wisdom shared by this group of writers. If your library doesn't already have a copy, request them to order it.

Being able to write and knowing how to self-publish is imperative for anyone trying to overcome our prison conditions. We need to get our thoughts and ideas out into society, using our minds to enlighten the public to our struggle. The majority of citizens see us as "less than human" but this is because we are strangers to them. Let's introduce ourselves, show the world who we are. At the same time let's NOT further crystallize the stereotype we're already presenting. Break the mold and do something different. Make your words into something organic, food that is good for your body, not junk or fast-food that only destroys.

Once you've finished up one of your works, and are ready to share it with the world, this is when execution becomes key. Here's a quick summary of what you'll need to do in order to self-publish and get your work into the market place.

Copyright Your Material (visit www.copyright.gov to copyright). No, the "ghetto copyright" will not hold up in court. It doesn't work. I remember people telling me to just mail my works home and tell my family to never open the envelope and, because the date from the envelope shows "when" it was mailed and the envelope has never been opened, my works had copyright protection. This is not true. Take the steps necessary to protect your work. It costs approximately $100 but you can file more than one work at a time under the same fee.

Here are the 7 Steps it takes to receive copyright protection, in the words of best-selling author, Dan Brown (The DaVinci Code, Angels and Demons, Inferno):

1. Visit the Official Copyright Website.

   Set up by the Library of Congress, copyright.gov is a site that allows you to fill out and submit registration forms online by completing a few simple steps of the registration process.

2. Select the Proper Category.

   Click where it says "Register a Copyright", then select "Literary Works".

3. Create an Online Account.

   If you don't already have an online account with the US. Copyright Office, create one to access the portal.

4. Select the Standard Application.

   Once you've logged into the site, navigate to the left side of the screen where it says "Register a Work". Beneath that, click where it reads "Standard Application".

5. Fill out the Appropriate Forms.

   Click "Start Registration", then complete the form with all the appropriate information regarding your book.

6. Pay the Fee

   Pay the U.S. Copyright Office filing fee.

7. Submit Your Written Material.

Send in the final polished version of your manuscript to the U.S. Copyright Office.

These 7 Steps came from Dan Brown's website www.masterclass.com a guide through the publication process.

Note: You cannot copyright the title of your book (but you can protect the book cover). The best thing to do once you're decided on the title of your book is to get a domain name as the title of your book. This costs approximately $10 a year but is a necessary step of protection. Visit www.porkbun.com to purchase your domain name for under $10.
ISBN # (visit www.myidentifier.org to purchase)

In America, books are required to have their own ISBN #, like their own little personal social security number. This is the number you see on the barcode on the back of books. You can purchase 10 ISBN #'s online for $295 (which provides for 10 different works) and maintain complete control over your rights of ownership and do as you please with your works. Many businesses will give you a free ISBN # but there's always something that comes with it..

Book Cover and Title

People DO judge books by their covers. Typically, you get what you pay for. A graphic designer will be required to finish this step, however, I'm about to share a gem with you I discovered in the finishing stages of writing this book. There's an app called ChatGPT. ChatGPT can generate images in seconds of ideas better than you imagined. For example, I asked ChatGPT to generate an image for me using the title of this book as its only frame of reference (because I was having a difficult time coming up with cover ideas of my own) and within seconds appeared my beautiful book cover. The image was emailed to me and my jaw dropped when I saw it. Artificial Intelligence read the title of my book and synthesized the concept. It was a good day for me. I knew that this was the one! I've been generating images on AI ever since. This is a new era of technology we're living in which makes life easier for some people, more difficult for others. A graphic designer would have charged me $500 for this image and still probably not have did as well. But you will still need to find and hire a graphic designer to alter the image by at least 30% to avoid any copyright infringements and to include the book's Title and Author name. This should cost you no more than $50 as all they're doing is designing font, not an image.

To find a graphic designer, and almost any other kind of help you may need for your works or business, I always refer people to Fiverr. If you haven't seen its commercials, Fiverr is an online platform of freelancers from all over the world who are looking to do work for you. It's an excellent resource to get almost anything done. Install the app or go to www.fiverr.com to find a graphic designer.

When the work is finished, always request the "source file" of your cover.

You'll want a catchy title for your work, of course. Remember to get the domain name as your book's title right away. Imagine if someone else had the website that was the title of your work? That's exactly what you do NOT want. Even if you don't plan on having a website, it's a smart business decision to protect your title with a domain name. (See SYO Business for a few websites that sell domain names).

Editors and Beta Readers

An editor is recommended for writers because you want someone other than yourself to polish up your work after you've finished it. You'll want that professional set of eyes to go over things and ensure it all makes sense and the message appears clear to the reader. As well as correcting spelling and grammatical errors, good editors clean up sentences and help paragraphs blend together. None of us are professional writers so it helps to have someone who will try to make it appear as if we are, in fact, professionals. Beta Reader's are people who will read over your work and usually assist by giving their opinions, offering suggestions, etc. They're here to help so we should take their criticisms into account.

Editors and Beta Readers can be found on Fiverr, as well as another freelance platform called www.upwork.com. Another good site for resources.www.goodreads.com.

Proof reading websites:

www.grammarly.com

www.slickwrite.com

www.proofreadbot.com

Freelance websites:

www.fiverr.com

www.upwork.com

www.freelances.com

Find Beta Readers at:

www.mywriterscircle.com

www.writing.com

Book Formatting

You can format your book yourself using Adobe InDesign but if you're having a hard time, look to Fiverr for assistance. Spend no more than $20 on this, as any one can do it. Determine what you want the size of your book to be, then format accordingly. Make sure everything looks exactly how you want it to because this is how it will print.

Metadata

Metadata is a set of smaller data (words) that describe and give information about other data. Basically, your metadata are keywords that search engines look for when deciding whether your work matches the customer's desire. Learning SEO (search engine optimization) helps with choosing the right terms to use, but it's all about matching your metadata with what you believe people are typing into Google or Amazon. When people are searching for a book, yours will be found based on the information you included when you uploaded your work to the self-publishing site. You're allowed 7 Keywords to use as your metadata, each keyword being separated by a comma. but here's a little secret... inside each bracket of keywords you are allowed 50-characters, which you can use wisely to optimize a search. An example of this strategy would be "how to self-publish how to publish a book". This phrase has 41-characters but has only one keyword. Use this strategy when deciding what to use as your metadata.

Your Book Title / Subtitle, as well as your book's Description, are all important for optimization as well. An example of a wise subtitle used for optimization is "For fans of Robert Greene and Don Webb". With this subtitle, anyone who searches these authors may now run across your works. The website www.adwords.google.com/KeywordPlanner is a great resource for optimizing metadata.

Marketing Plan

Simply uploading your works to Amazon's bookstore doesn't mean that people will see it. You'll need a marketing plan to get your work in front of the public. Advertisement is the only way to increase sales and bring attention to your work and it cannot be ignored. Of course, getting your work to be available on Amazon is the first step, but marketing is the important second. Once you decide on a title for your work, purchase a domain name. Use your book cover to create marketing tools. There are many different ways to advertise your products. Be creative! Make t-shirts, book marks, YouTube videos, Tiktok and other social media platforms, business cards, banners, etc. As an inmate, do not waste time or money on a publicist. Promote yourself! Become the face of your brand!

Having your own website is a great way to market, as well as give yourself credibility as a professional. It's important for inmates because people are automatically leery of dealing with us. A website is more credible than a social media page (although social media is imperative, obviously).

Another benefit to having your own website is it can be utilized to capture and design a customer mailing list. While developing an audience, a mailing list is a major component. MailChimp is a service that links to a website, designed to capture people's e-mail address.

You can design your own website via WordPress, Shopify, or Wix. I've used Shopify myself (as previously mentioned) which is user friendly and relatively cheap. WordPress is free and is a great resource once learn how to use it. Tutorials are available on YouTube and Google. Our websites   (morethananinmate.com,   bestselfpublications.com   and morethananinmatesgirlfriend.com) were all made using WordPress.

Blogs and promotional videos are another excellent tool of marketing. Advertisement methods are unlimited, a lifestyle of its own. I've seen a guy purchase a billboard off the interstate for 30-days and posted a picture of himself and his book cover for everybody to see as they drove to/from work. You can utilize pen pal websites or Facebook dating in the same way by posting pictures of you book covers and advertise like that. Purchase ad segments from newsletters like Criminal Legal News and Prison Legal News, magazines, podcasts etc. Ask fans to support your work by making Tiktok videos of them with your book, speaking highly of it. Give free copies of your works to social media influencers, prison libraries, real libraries, gas stations or corner stores, etc. I'm trying to get my works in front of as many people as I can. I recommend you to do the same. See chapter SYO Business for an exhausted list of marketing weapons.

I wish you the best in your endeavors! If you've decided to take up writing and are looking to network, hit me up. I'm always open to meeting new business partners, especially with those who share my struggle. If you write and are having trouble getting your works to the public, I can help with that too. Just reach out.

My final two gems I'll leave you with concerning writing and self-publishing...

<u>Utilize the Public Domain.</u> The public domain is a world full of works that have no copyright protections, or whose protections have expired. Whatever belongs to the public domain "belongs to the public" meaning that anybody can capitalize from these works. Anything can be found and used, from entire books, to images and artwork, symbols and signs to reports and government publications. Nothing considered a "fact" can be copyrighted (such as everything in your Almanac). Only "the way in which the fact is expressed" can receive copyright protection. You can rewrite any

factual book in your own words and sell it yourself. You can rewrite books that are classics like Frankenstein, Dr. Jekyl and Mr. Hyde, Might is Right, the Bible itself if you wanted to! You can find images, add your company name to it and copyright that, then turn that image into your business logo! Game is unlimited within the public domain.

<u>OCR programs</u>. Optical Character Recognition. Have a manuscript wrote out but can't find anybody who will help you type it on Microsoft Word and convert to a PDF file? No problem! Technology is here to save the day. I was having this problem for years and it was a major roadblock in the way of getting my works to the market. Getting my manuscripts typed was such a major issue for me that I began losing faith in my own dreams. But I kept at it, kept writing. Then we discovered an app that knocked the road block completely out of my way. There are several similar to it but the one we've been using is called "Handwriting to Text recognition". This app allows someone to take a picture of the page of your handwriting and convert it to text a second later, which you can then copy/paste to Microsoft Word. And it works like a charm! A real blessing to inmate writers who have shared in this struggle. Not too many people are willing to take time out of their day for weeks at a time - but now all they've got to do is take a picture of each of your pages. Your entire manuscript can be typed and converted to a PDF file within an hour or two... with no typing involved. Between the

"Handwriting to Text recognition" app and "ChatGPT" I've saved about $1,000 per book and is less work for my network team. Gems.

"Tonight" by Agha Shahd Ali.

Where are you now? Who lies beneath your spell

Whom else from rapture's road will you expel tonight?

Those "Fabrics of Cashmere—" "to make Me beautiful—"

"Trinket"—to gem—"Me to adorn—How tell"—tonight?

I beg for haven: Prisons, let open your gates—

A refugee from Belief seeks a cell tonight.

God's vintage loneliness has turned to vinegar—

All the archangels—their wings frozen—fell tonight.

Lord, cried out the idols, Don't let us be broken;

Only we can convert the infidel tonight.

Mughal ceilings, let your mirrored convexities

multiply me at once under your spell tonight.

He's freed some fire from ice in pity for Heaven.

He's left open—for God—the doors of Hell tonight.

In the heart's veined temple, all statues have been smashed.

No priest in saffron's left to toll its knell tonight.

God, limit these punishments, there's still Judgment Day—

I'm a mere sinner, I'm no infidel tonight.

Executioners near the woman at the window.

Damn you, Elijah, I'll bless Jezebel tonight.

The hunt is over, and I hear the Call to Prayer

fade into that of the wounded gazelle tonight.

My rivals for your love—you've invited them all?

This is mere insult, this is no farewell tonight.

And I, Shahid, only am escaped to tell thee—

God sobs in my arms. Call me Ishmael tonight.

Pen Pals

Although physically encaged next to hundreds of people, prisons are still one of the loneliest places on earth. This loneliness comes from being taken away from your family, your friends, your associates, your neighbors, the land you grew up on, peers and nature - from having been removed from the entire life you know and locked inside a concrete building. Everyone in here craves the life that is now behind them, and because our fellow inmates weren't a part of that life and crave to get back to their own, they don't alleviate the loneliness. We all feel it, we all get it, but most times our imprisonment is the only thing we have that relates to each other. We're all so different. We share in these struggles together but each of us is doing our own number, our own prison bid.

What I've found to be one of the most meaningful passages of growth is the opportunity for me to reach out to the world via pen pal sites and people... people I'd have never met had I never came to prison, new friends, new associates, possibly even new romantic partners. Meeting and associating with new people from the community helps us break away from old patterns of thinking and acting while growing into a new person. We're all influenced by our peers, whether we'd like to believe so or not. Meeting new people, especially those who are loving, caring, and positive can be life-altering. It has been for me.

There's something transformative about the effect of a woman who you've never met before your imprisonment deciding to hold you down and be there for you through your darkest days, your lowest moments- especially when the people you've known from your old life have jumped ship and abandoned you, or simply moved on and left you in the past. Not many things feel worst than when the people you love leave you while you're down and move on with their lives. It's traumatic and difficult, we've all dealt with it and fought to get on with our lives - sometimes to no prevail. Sometimes even this can be transformative, everyone handles life differently.

But as bad as it feels to experience these people leave is as good as it feels to have new ones reach out to be supportive. The universe can work in mysterious ways. I've seen guys meet their wives from behind these walls, get out and go home to a new family and a new way of life that they never imagined being possible. I've seen guys meet women from different countries who love them so much that they move their entire lives here to be with them (as well as from other states). There's TV shows about this kind of thing, like Prison Brides and Love After Lockup.

I've also witnessed the transformative effect that love and support had on these men, giving them extra strength to grow into better people. One thing about it... we should all be trying to meet new people, all the time. It should remain one of our priorities. Meeting new people is a key step to networking, as well as spreading our image to more people. The more people that know us and recognize our integrity, the more people are willing to fight for us - even if that "fight" is simply their vote supporting prison reform or them speaking a positive opinion about inmates, which may be influenced by them knowing you. The more people who are influenced by our positive character, the more voices we have for social change. It's important that we always meet new people. Networking is a priority.

But how is it that we meet new people from behind bars ? Surprisingly, there are many ways for us to meet people and network with others, especially as more and more people are beginning to see the need for social change and noticing the inhumane conditions we're living in. The most obvious way to meet someone is through word of mouth. Basically, asking your fellow prisoners to see if any of their women have any friends who would be interested in a pen pal. Or, family/friends from the free world telling people they know that you're looking for a pen pal. We've probably all already tried this method. Sometimes it works, most of the time it doesn't. But if the opportunity presents itself, you should take it.

Another way to meet new people is to get a list of addresses to your local churches from your religious coordinators. Write these churches, explaining a little bit about yourself, who you are and what your intentions are. Churches are already working for social change so they are good groups of people to network with, most of them having morals and integrity of their own. A bible verse that many people know is: *"For I was hungry and you gave me something to eat, I was thirsty and you gave me something to drink.. I was in prison and you came to visit me."* - Matthew 25:35-36

Churches have always been supportive of prisoners. Recall how many characters of the Bible were imprisoned and persecuted by the system. John the Baptist was imprisoned and beheaded; Ignatius was imprisoned and fed to lions; but the goat was Saint Paul, who, from his prison cell, created the largest network system of all prisoners as he wrote his epistles (letters) to the world. These letters became the majority of the New Testament after his death- and they were wrote from behind bars. One-third of the world lives by the words Paul wrote from in his cell. The churches have never forgotten their history and are supportive of the struggles we face daily. Reach out with a genuine heart and you will receive pen pals.

The most popular way to network and meet new people is to actually post an ad onto pen pal or dating sites. There are hundreds of these sites nowadays but the two most popular (and efficient) pen pal sites for incarcerated people are Write A Prisoner and Meet An Inmate. Write A Prisoner receives over 5,000 views per day and Meet An Inmate over 4,000. They're kind of a big deal in the field of meeting people. Combined, a total of 9,000 people from across the world will see your profile every day, according to statistics, and both of these sites have been successful for myself and many others. The websites are www.writeaprisoner.com and www.meet-an-inmate.com - I suggest you invest the money into these sites. Yes, they cost money. And yes, I say "invest" because that's what it is... an investment into your happiness, your network team, and your actions toward social change. It's worth it. I've learned that the best times of the year to upload your profile is when the summer ends and it starts getting cold outside. You know how people are in the summer, and you know how people are in the winter - so it only makes sense that we'll receive more pen pals during the winter season.

Write A Prisoner charges $65 for a 1,500 - character bio and allows you to upload one picture. The ad stays on the site for a year.

Meet An Inmate charges $45 for a 1,500-character bio, which allows you to upload two pictures and places your ad on the home-page so that when first posted, it receives lots of views. However, the ad only stays on the site for 6-months. There's really not much difference between whether your ad is up for 6-months or one-year because you're going to receive most of your pen pals in the first 3-months. After that, your ad is basically lost in the ocean of profiles.

Both of these sites take the time to verify your charges that you're incarcerated for and how much time you're serving. Be honest in your bio, try to be as genuine as possible. Here's an example of a bio, an introduction I've used for both of these sites:

<u>Pen Pal Profile Example</u>

Email App: Getting Out

Name: Nicholas Ely

Inmate #077049

State: Nebraska

Facility / Prison: Reception and Treatment Center

33, Blue eyes / Brown hair. I'm pretty tall, 6'4" with a slim build. I'm white, I have tattoos that cover my arms and body (But I'm not toxic, I promise!) Looking to meet a woman I can vibe with... Someone who has it in em to accept the kinda man I am. One of my fav song lyrics goes "if I told you I was different, would you understand the difference?" Do I see myself as different from other men?... Yeah, I'm one of a kind! (But I'm not a narcissist, I promise!) I'd appreciate an opportunity to get to know you and all the things that make you different from other women. But fr, I'm just looking for a woman I can spend some time with, share some life with, connect with... and maybe even trust.

You should know that I've been in here for the last 13 years, since I was 20, and that somehow I landed myself a natural life sentence. I've never really accepted that this is it for me and have remained optimistic that my appeal will set me free again some day. It's complicated but I'm innocent. If you have any questions about it, feel free to ask.

Some days are easier than others, but every day I try to make a good day. Life is too short for anything else. I'm a good man, one of integrity. Take a chance and let me show you. I'm an open book, easy going, and will accept you for you. Email me.

There are other pen pal websites for inmates, similar to the aforementioned, but I won't include them here because I have personally never used them or heard of anybody else using them. If you've happened to use any other ones and received success, let me know!

For those who don't have the money to be spending on pen pal sites, don't lose hope... there are other options that are free and may work just as well. Even if you do post an ad on a website you've paid for, still take advantage of these opportunities available on social media.

If TikTok is still legal by the time this book makes it into your hands, you need to utilize it. It has the most efficient algorithm that spreads videos directly to the people who want to see them! I mean, they're spying on you... they should know what you want to see, right? Not only does their spying give them a competitive edge, but sharing videos with potential pen pals can be better than photos... especially for those of us who aren't photogenic. Sometimes a picture just doesn't capture the essence you'd like to share, your swag, and a picture can't catch your charisma. That little video clip might catch the eye of someone who would bypass your photo...and they get to hear your voice. Just try not to make an idiot of yourself. Again, keep it simple and genuine.

If you can't record a video at your facility (or if you just don't want to) you can still share your photo on TikTok with your contact information. I've seen that work too.

My state's prisons are behind on any/all technological advancements so we just started receiving video visits on Zoom within the last two years. During video visits is when/where we'd make our introductory video. All we do is have our visitor hit the "record screen" button that all smart phones have and make ourselves a little video. I'd suggest anywhere from 10-30 seconds, no longer. Have your contact info already on the screen or included in the video's description, that way you don't have to waste time talking about how to get ahold of you.

To spread your video on Tik Tok, you must use the "hashtag" feature that we're all so familiar with. When uploading the video, there will be a box available for you to describe your video or comment about it. Within this space you must hashtag all of the different pen pal pages, as well as the tag FYP (For Your Page). These hashtags will help spread your video to the most people. The description section of your video should

include your contact information, as well as these tags:

#writeaprisoner
#prisonpenpals
#penpalswanted
#prisonertok
#prisonmate
#wap

And watch your video spread like wild fire! TikTok also shows

how many people have viewed your video so you'll be able to keep track,

for whatever reason. Your TikTok must be public, NOT private.

I'm not as familiar with Instagram but I know that it has pages

dedicated to helping inmates meet pen pals. They let you share 10-second

"reels" (videos) as well but the majority of Instagram users post pictures.

Have your people type write a prisoner into the search bar and they will

appear. Someone who reached out to me had shared with me that her and

her friends were playing a drinking game using Instagram and prison pen

pal reels... the rules of the game were you watch a video and then guess

what they were in for. If you were wrong, you drink. Either she took too

many shots that night or somebody caught her eye... but the point is that

she found her way to me via Instagram.

What's interesting to me is that the majority of pen pals I met on

this last post were somehow led to my ad by TikTok or Instagram. These are two very powerful social media platforms that led new people to me... and I've never even used them! I've never posted any pen pal ads on either of them, but they both advertise Write A Prisoner and Meet An Inmate to anyone their algorithm deems interested.

And, of course, we can't forget about those of us who still use their Facebook (billions of people). Yes, our family/friends can share with their family/friends that you're looking for a pen pal, but I'm speaking of the community groups. There are dozens of different groups designed to match prisoners with pen pals. As with TikTok and Instagram, somebody you know will need to have an account and will need to post your ad for you, but most of us know someone with a FB.

Here's how it works...

1) Have someone go to Facebook and click "Facebook Groups"

2) Type into the search bar "Prison Pen Pals".

3) Facebook will list dozens of these groups, the best ones (because they have the most members) are "Write a Prisoner" and "Prison Pen Pals", but all of them are good.

4) Your someone must join the group before being allowed to place an ad, which takes about 24-hours to be accepted.

5) Once accepted, place your ad into a post (pictures and an intro, maybe some videos) and share with the community.

That's it! Your post will then appear on the news feed of over 10,000 people across the world, if not more. They're obviously part of the group because they're interested in being a pen pal, or, they've posted people on the pages before - but even that's cool. My sister met the now father-of-her-child/fiancé through one of these pages while posting an ad for me several years ago. You never know whose eye you might catch or who you might meet.

Here's an example of the ad my sister had shared for me in a few different groups:

Email App: Getting Out

Name: Nicholas Ely

Number 077049

State: Nebraska

Facility/Prison: Reception and Treatment Center

My name is Nicholas Ely, 33 years old.

Being in my room 21-hours a day, I have lots of free time on my hands. most of it being spent reading, writing, and exercising. The last few years I've been focused on bettering myself as a man, reflecting on where I went wrong in life, and adapting to my living conditions... but lately I've been craving a connection with someone from the outside world again. I have no expectations from anyone, I'd just like to get to know you and hear about life. I'm an open book and a good listener.

Somehow, I've found myself serving a life sentence for something I didn't do, but I remain hopeful that through my appeal I will be free again someday.

My sister has posted this ad for me so if you'd like to email me but have anything you'd like to know about me before reaching out, send her a message and she'll be more than happy to help. Have a good day.

It doesn't need to be anything too jazzy or drastic. I don't ever go for the whole "bad boy" image, you don't need to advertise that you're a gangster or intimidating. Most people are already intimidated by us simply because we're in prison. It's better to be warm and welcoming, smile in your photographs, appear humane and humble. That's what I've noticed works best for me.

I had a friend place an ad on Facebook groups using videos of himself working out in his cell, covered in baby oil! (captured using a cell phone) Sounds funny, but those damn things went viral, receiving over 3 million views! Bro blew up the internet! And he received thousands of emails from people, some of them being lawyers who wanted to work on his appeal for him (as he is a lifer). Women made memes using his videos, and other sites such as TMZ and The Shade shared them as well. We had no idea that shit would take off like that... but you never know what could happen until you try.

If you don't have anyone who will post your ad on these social media pages or place your ad onto the websites... don't use that as an excuse to not get yourself out there. Hundreds of inmates around you DO have people that will help you get this done, especially if you're a man of integrity. Some charge you a fee for their help, but that's fine. You should want to pay them for their assistance any ways. There are millions of hustles one can do in prison to run up $100 to invest into getting yourself on these pages. If you don't get yourself out there in front of the world, nobody will know you're a prisoner or searching for pen pals. People out there want to write you but it's your responsibility to make yourself available. Do what you gotta do to be seen. Don't ignore these opportunities.

Be Somebody with something to offer. Don't seek to meet new people in the hopes of finding someone you can use for money and visits. That shit aint cool, that shit is not a "hustle" – it's childish mentality. Just think about the nature between man and woman. The man has always been the protector and provider, the woman being the lover and caretaker of the home. I know that society doesn't always agree with this narrative anymore but it is still our nature as humans. There's nothing "manly" about living off of women, and you'll feel better about yourself as a man when you have your own. We've got to shatter the stigma of inmates just trying to use women... it's not a good look, especially because this scares away good women. Men of integrity aren't aiming to use women; we're aiming to "build" with people. There's a major difference between the two, and both can assist you in achieving your goals. Choose the path of integrity. Help us shatter the stigmas used to imprison us. Always have something to offer the relationship, even if that something to offer is simply a listening ear. Women feel loved when they're heard, when they're listened to. Men feel loved when we're respected. Genuinely listen to a woman and she will respect you.

Listening does not mean problem solve. Women aren't stupid; they don't need us to solve any of their problems for them. They just want to know that you are there. Most of the time we think women are telling us their problems because they'd like us to solve it for them. Fix it, handle the situation. But this isn't true. Women want to tell you about their lives, as well as the things that are bothering them, and they want you to simply listen-making them feel assured that you care about them, their lives, their feelings and thoughts. When listening, don't always shoot back a response which you believe will solve the problem. That's how men communicate with men, but not how we should communicate with women. Just be there for them and actively listen. Don't offer advice (to anyone) unless you're asked for it. Sometimes the hardest thing for us to offer is a listening ear, but as the saying goes.... *"We were given two ears and one mouth because we're suppose to listen twice as much as we speak."* That's a little piece of gold to assist you in your endeavors.

Again... Women ain't stupid. Another reason why a man of integrity shouldn't try to play women or be dishonest is because these days there are way too many ways to catch you up. A note for those who are still struggling with old habits, women who talk to prisoners have traps set up all over the internet, specifically social media. I've mentioned Facebook and how they can assist you in meeting people, but these groups are used for other things as well. They're a great tool for people to get together and socialize, network and such. Groups are used to "share information with each other"... you see where I'm going with this? Women scorned by inmates have created their own FB groups designed to catch up men in prison. There are dozens of these groups, each of them having thousands of female members... suspicious women who make posts with the caption. "Is anybody else talking to this inmate?" with pictures of you attached. Women from all over the world receive these posts directly to their news feed and can verify whether they're man is talking to other women. There are entire groups designed for the only purpose of posting "Are you talking to my man?" captions. I've seen numerous men get caught up through these groups.

Other groups are designed for women to share all of an inmate's emails and conversations they've had with each other once she's deemed him a "playa" or "user" (or if she's just crazy, which is sometimes the case). When a woman convinces herself she's "being used" she can post your personal photos, emails and letters, with the caption "This man is a scumbag. We've been talking for 9 months and the entire time he's been using me for money while still talking to his baby mama." Then thousands of women all over the world receive these posts about you. Not only is this a horrible image for a man of integrity, it's detrimental in our fight for freedom and prison reform. We don't want to add to society's belief that we are bad people who deserve prison. Our mission is to fight against this stigma, not feed it fuel.

Overall, I get it. I'm just like you and have been there, done that. But recognize the error in this behavior, visualize the bigger picture, see the harm this causes us. I'm fully aware that women aren't perfect angels - I've had my fair share of little demons - but I'm asking you to be the bigger man. Be the man, a man- don't scoop to the level of other people's bullshit. Don't be influenced by peers who believe it's acceptable behavior to misuse people. *Be the change you want to see in the world*. If you want to see women be loyal and faithful, be a loyal and faithful man. Don't tell yourself, "I know she's out there fuckin' so Ima..." as a way to justify acting out of character. Stop acting out of natural character and stop making excuses that you believe justify negativity. You don't fight fire with fire... you fight it with water. Don't see women as the enemy… that don't even sound right. We've all been hurt by women in the past, women have been hurt by us and other men. Let's not hold the next one accountable for somebody else's mistakes - especially when they're reaching out to you in prison, standing by you at your lowest moments. Remember; *men of integrity.*

We're not in a position to be turning down love from anybody, I do understand that. But I also believe that when someone truly loves or cares about you, they will never let you go without- for any reason. Just don't misuse people.

So.. as there are groups designed to catch people up, there are also groups designed to build people up, motivate and inspire relationships with someone in prison. One of these groups is called "Prisoner Love Journeys" which serves as a community for women who remain dedicated to their men in prison. Many people in society don't understand or agree with why they would be with a prisoner and, because they don't understand, will be unaccepting ... may even judge or shame her. Because of this negativity, women have developed a sisterhood within groups like Prison Love Journeys where they're all supportive of each other. An example of this was when my girl (at the time) who I had just recently became serious with had done everything she could to get a ride to come see me in visits.

We had never met "in person" yet and it seemed as if she wasn't going to make it to the visit. We had both been looking forward to finally meeting each other and were devastated. But, after expressing her sadness about it on "Prison Love Journeys", a woman from our State (who my girl didn't know) sent her a comment offering to give her a ride to come see me. We couldn't believe it and were more than thankful...we felt blessed. And I was able to meet her for the first time that week. It was a hell of an experience which only happened because of positive groups online like that one.

There are also groups designed to support inmate's businesses. Like, maybe a prisoner is an excellent artist who uses pastels to draw beautiful portraits - I've seen women help sell artwork through these groups. Or, women who make Free YSL t-shirts who will personalize items of clothing for other women who have men in prison. It's just neat to experience people coming together in support of inmates. These opportunities were never available to us as of 10 years ago... but now they are.

Reach out to the world, network with us!

I'm always down to network and communicate - reach out to me if you want to. I'll write back. Iron sharpens Iron. Men of Integrity.

Chief Tecumseh's poem

So live your life that the fear of death can never enter your heart.

Trouble no one about their religion; respect others in their view,

and demand that they respect yours.

Love your life, perfect your life, beautify all things in your life.

Seek to make your life long and its purpose in the service of your people.

Prepare a noble death song for the day when you go over the great divide.

Always give a word or a sign of salute when meeting or passing a friend,

even a stranger, when in a lonely place.

Show respect to all people and grovel to none.

When you arise in the morning give thanks for the food and for the joy of

living.

If you see no reason for giving thanks, the fault lies only in yourself.

Abuse no one and no thing,

for abuse turns the wise ones to fools and robs the spirit of its vision.

When it comes your time to die,

be not like those whose hearts are filled with the fear of death,

so that when their time comes they weep and pray for a little more time

to live their lives over again in a different way.

Sing your death song and die like a hero going home."

PART THREE

Blog Post #1- April 6, 2020

If you don't know me personally, you may not know that I am currently serving a prison sentence of life without parole. My conviction is being appealed, and I plan on coming home some day. I maintain that I am innocent, and trust that our legal system will fix its error.

No, I didn't make the smartest decisions when I was 18 and 20, but not many of us do. Some peoples' mistakes are worst than others, but we all have committed acts of stupidity at this age. Over the last 10 years, I've did a lot of reflecting and have made dramatic changes within myself, and can say with confidence that I am no longer the man I was back then. I dream of being released back into society, where I can finally show my friends and loved ones that I've become, and will remain, a "productive" member of our society, rather than a "destructive" one. Nobody is the same person they were 10 years ago, and if you are, then you've wasted 10 years of your life. I have not wasted and I spend my time reading, writing, studying, and providing myself with an education. I believe that ignorance (lack of education) is the cause for many people's mistakes that lead them to where I'm at, and if I truly want to remain free once I'm released, I know education is the answer. Sadly, our prison systems do not offer any form of education past receiving your high school diploma, so we must take it upon ourselves. I've participated in every "class" that prison claims to offer, and have even developed a class for the social workers to use called "Upon Release". Everyday I work on rehabilitating myself.

I'm sharing this information with you in hopes that people can look past my case and see me for the man I really am. People probably don't think of me often, but if the thought of me ever does cross their minds, I don't want it to be "he's got a life sentence, what a waste". My time is not being wasted, and things happen in our lives for particular reasons. I am still a human being, no matter how long I've been incarcerated. I live, breath, hurt, and smile, every day. Yes, my body is in prison, but my mind remains free.

I know how it feels to be forgotten. The world mourns, forgets, and moves on with life, which is only natural. I blame no one for the mistakes I made in my past, and I blame no one for me being where I'm at. I take responsibility for my success as well as for my failures. But, I ask for people to look beyond the mistakes made by prisoners, and instead try to view them by the changes they've made within themselves while incarcerated. In a country where our prison system's foundation was built around a "warehouse" philosophy, (basically just a place to house people who have violated policy), rather than being built around a process of rehabilitation, its quite amazing and surprising to witness some of the changes people make on their own free cognition. There is no process instilled within our prison system that allows for one to receive adequate rehabilitative programs, and the lack of community ties only makes the problem worst. Studies show that inmates who have strong bonds and relationships with members in our society are much less likely to re-offend upon release.

If you know anyone who is incarcerated that has shown they're attempting to change and become a better person, reach out to let them know that our society supports those people willing to reform, that we support "change", and that each individual is more than an inmate. You'd be surprised how much a simple email or letter could make somebody's entire week so much better. You never know what kind of effect that your "reaching out" could have on an incarcerated person. You may provide the hope required for someone to find that goodness within themselves and create a positive change within our society.

"No matter how much you change, you still have to pay the price for the things you've done."

We understand that. We just ask that you see the person, not the statistic.

Thank you for your time. Have a wonderful day

Blog Post #2 – July 12, 2021

America is home to a little under 5% of the world's entire human population, but houses over 20% of the worlds inmate population! Those are staggering numbers, but the statistic is true. What does this statistic mean? It means that American tax dollars are spent on warehouses being used to 'store people' (as opposed to 'rehabilitate'), and that there is a serious need for prison reform in the States. I believe this change would occur if society was provided an opportunity to see for themselves what is really happening within America's prison system, and to see where their tax dollars are being annually wasted.

You would imagine the purpose of a prison would be to punish and/or rehabilitate, but this is an incorrect (although logical) assumption. Prisons are not designed to punish nor rehabilitate humans, but are created to pacify people until their release date, thus, our 67% recidivism rate. Then, when a criminal comes home and reoffends again, we question (nobody specifically) ''Did he not learn anything while he was in prison last time?'' And the simple but sad answer is: No, he did not learn anything while incarcerated, and, he did not learn anything (for the most part) because this system does not offer any opportunity to learn anything, any opportunity to education or means of rehabilitation. An inmate comes to prison and has nothing productive that he can do to fulfill his time, so he spends all day being further conditioned by other criminals/gang members, playing cards or watching Jerry Springer and Maury until he is released again. And the cycle continues.

This is not a plea for help or sympathy, nor an individual complaint, but is my attempt to paint you a picture that captures the essence of our judicial systems failures.

There will be many of you who say "A person has free will and can blame nobody but themselves for any decision they've made, and that they deserve to be punished as a consequence of their irresponsible actions.'' And I will tell you that I agree 100% with this belief. Each of us do have a free will to act (as we should) thus it's only logical that we must punish those who infringe upon the freedoms and security of others. But, I don't believe because somebody has made a bad decision in their past (maybe even a horrible one) that they are incapable of change. Change is not a simple process, and we all know how difficult it is to break what have become habits in life. But, because it is a difficult process and a rare accomplishment, the system fails to try. They simply, warehouse. Thus, who can we point the finger at?

Well, it can only be an inmate, of course. So, what if an inmate who rehabilitates and educates HIMSELF while he's inside, even without help from the state, who has no incentive to change but does so because he truly desires it and wants a better life for himself; is willing to put in the work and devotion required of redemption, to be persistent in the face of struggles and overcome any obstacles or temptations along the way. What of the inmate who has reflected upon his past and recognized the errors, eradicated them from his character completely, has purified his being, but… is never coming home. I don't have an easy answer for any of it, but I know a conversation helps. There are people within these prison walls that are More Than An Inmate, and some of them may never receive a second chance at life, but are still working everyday to become better people.

More Than An Inmate seeks to give a voice to those who are lost in the system but diligently working to make a positive change for themselves, and, in effect, their community.

More Than An Inmate is a brand that represents those inmates who no longer live the life of a criminal, who have spent their time educating themselves and have taken the necessary steps to become rehabilitated citizens, preparing to become productive members of society upon release. We represent the inmates who recognize the error of their past indiscretions and have developed a lifestyle of integrity, honesty, and empathy since being incarcerated. More Than An Inmate is for those who look around their prison setting and identify the difference in character between them and their fellow inmates, understanding that 'I no longer belong in a place like this.' We represent those who are never the same man today that they were yesterday, and will wake up tomorrow a changed man again; for those of us who truly feel remorseful for the pain we've caused others, and believe that there is no place in our societies for the people that we once were. And finally, we represent the loved ones of those who are More Than An Inmate, who see a goodness and potential behind the walls, and have shown their support even when times were difficult.

Who am I?

My name is Nicholas, and I am the founder of the More Than An Inmate organization. I am currently an inmate incarcerated in the State of Nebraska prison system, but as our name suggests, I see myself as more than that. I am a flesh and blood person, just like you, except for the fact that I spend 14 hours of my day locked inside of an 8' by 14' cell (a bathroom that is used as a bedroom to house two full grown men.) I am passionate about reading and writing, and I believe that the power of words and a conversation can inspire real change.

I am here introducing More Than An Inmate to you in hopes that we can build a genuine relationship with society again. I know some may feel that we do not deserve a second opportunity; I respect the beliefs and views of others, and a beautiful thing about our society is that we're all entitled to our own opinions. I'm aware that my past decisions have caused irreparable damage, and I've accepted the fact that I deserve to be punished for the things that I've done….. but I also believe in the blind equality and fairness that Lady Justice is here to symbolize.

Blog Post #3- July 22, 2021

This is not my home.

This is not my home.

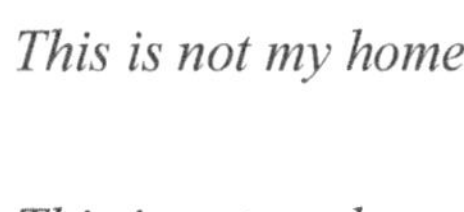

This is not my home.

This is not my home.

It feels like a mantra I have to tell myself to remember that this cell is not my house, this desk is not my dinner table, and this mattress is not my comforter bed. After 12 years, sometimes I can't remember that I had a life before all of this and that there is such a thing called freedom and society. I can't imagine how it must feel for people like my cellie who have spent more than 40 years incarcerated. He once told me that he feels like he was born here, and I'm starting to feel like that as well. I don't like the feeling, although recognizing prison with a sense of familiarity helps as a defense against the truth…the truth that I am in prison, and that if things don't change, I am never coming home.

That I'm being held accountable for the death of a 25-year-old man that I never knew, and that the actions I'm accused of committing have caused pain to so many people whom I'll never know. That these actions have caused unimaginable pain and misery to a mother and sister who have lost their beloved son and big brother. And that I'm being punished for actions that, by law, I've been found guilty of committing. That my momma is now 50-years-old and will continue to age, and that my brother who was 2 when I left is now 12, my sister who was 16 is now 26, and my niece who wasn't even born yet is now 8…and that each of them live their lives having accepted I'm never coming home from prison. This is all my brother and niece know for me, and of course my momma and sister WANT me to come home, but their hopes have been crushed too many times in the past already. It's much easier for them to just accept what is reality…

I'm serving a Life sentence, natural life, without the possibility of parole, for a murder that I didn't commit nor assist, for actions that were not recklessly indifferent to human life, but all the same, I'm serving Life. This is my last shot at an appeal, and if I don't win during this stage of things, then it's over for me. The only remaining hope I'll have left is that someday the sentence of "natural life" will be ruled as an unconstitutionally cruel and inhumane punishment, or that the State abolish the "felony murder" law (which holds people criminally liable for a murder they never committed, assisted, nor intended to occur). Either one will allow me to come home to my loved ones again someday, and that's all I can ask for in this life.

When I look back over the events that have happened, I feel pain, sorrow, and remorse for the victim's family. I could never begin to say I know the pain and suffering that they have felt and still feel to this day. There is a hole in my heart, carved by the events of the past, and I never expect his mother or sister to forgive any of us. I wouldn't forgive any of whom I believed caused the death of my loved ones so I could never expect them to either. I lay here at 11pm typing this on my tablet, still not understanding the effect my actions have, and I don't know if I ever truly will. When I think of how one small action can alter the course of a million lives, I realize there are no such things as small actions. Every decision we ever make is subject to the laws of cause and effect, and we always must be careful with every decision we ever make because it is impossible to foresee what effect our actions are subject to.

These days I contemplate every decision before it's made, down to the minute details, as I'm fully aware that the consequences of my actions (even if unintended) will be carried on my shoulders. If I could remove the pain and suffering from everyone's lives in the snap of a finger, of course I would do that... but I can't say that I would altar the course my life has taken, in any way, as this struggle has carved the man I am today. These scars have taught me lessons that I value and have led me to discover the precious wonders of the small things in life, the beauty that comes in a prepackaged gift that life offers each and every one of us, the rich happiness that can be felt during what appears to be impoverished suffering, that there is reason behind all things for those who allow themselves a purpose.

These events have led me to be introduced to the love of my life, who is my balance and my stability, my joy and my happiness, my life and my purpose, and I would never want anything other. These circumstances have led me to see how genuine the love from family can possibly be and that family are the ones from whom love is always real. My family, my unit, my tribe…they love me unconditionally now as they always have and they always will, and I return the same love. Family is what matters, and I could never see that I already had the family love I was always searching for, and they had been right in front of me the whole time, with me at every turn. As troubled and broken up as we are and have been, we've still always been a family that remains together on the other end of the struggles and pursuits. I've been away for a long time now, and through all the pain, grief, and stress that I've caused, they have always been here with me.

No…this is not my home.

Blog Post #4- August 1, 2021

The things people deal with while in a relationship with an incarcerated person… one thing for sure, it's not always simple. Relationships involving an incarcerated person endure 10 times as many problems and difficulties than do 'normal' relationships. Having unrealistic expectations of a partner is one cause of these problems, and not trusting your partner is another major one. A lot of times, a man goes to prison and expects his woman to put her life on hold for him… which is never a realistic possibility. That's not to say she can't be with him and be loyal to him the entire number (which she should if she loves him) but this doesn't mean that she must act as if she is in prison too!

For example, today my girlfriend went over to her friend's house (a friend whom she rarely visits as they are both adult mothers who have their own lives), and they decide to have a drink together while they discuss life and reminisce. They end up drinking a bit too much and she falls asleep on her couch. I'm trying to call and can't get ahold of her for almost 4 hours, which had me upset and borderline worried. Eventually, I get through and she tells me exactly what happened. Naturally, I'm pissed and tell her that I don't believe any of it… though in reality, I believe every word. I can't just snap out of my feelings, and it takes time to iron out the wrinkles of my thoughts. A relationship must be founded on trust while you're incarcerated, pure unshakeable trust, and sometimes it is difficult for both parties. I trust my girlfriend 100% and if I didn't, I wouldn't be with her. There's just no other alternative to a healthy relationship while in prison.

But anyways, she said something small that made me think about 'prison relationships'. She said 'Baby, the only thing that would have been different, is IF you were home I would have come home and fell asleep on the couch NEXT TO YOU. The only thing that's truly upsetting you is not being able to actually see me come home and fall asleep on the couch.' And I realized that she is absolutely right. She didn't say this in a condescending way, and her sincerity was enlightening to me. Every time that her and I have ever argued it has always been over something which wouldn't exist if I wasn't incarcerated. She never blames me for being here, she chooses to be in this relationship with me, and we are both conscious of the difficulties we will face while making our relationship work while I'm incarcerated. Both parties must be understanding of each other and be fully committed to dealing with the trivial, petty incidents that may arise while a partner is incarcerated. Now, in my example, my girlfriend was very apologetic and had sympathy for what I had dealt with and for the thoughts running through my head, and she apologized over and over for falling asleep… but what it all boils down to is that she had nothing to apologize for. She had did nothing wrong, and was simply living her life. She was still sorry, but I was not upset with her, and I told her that if she could replay that night I wouldn't want her to change a thing.

We have to be capable of trust in order for any real relationship to work (whether with a party incarcerated or not), and I trust my girlfriend. Trust is what allows a couple to not feel restraint, and to allow each other to live without feeling like they're walking on eggshells. Integrity to ones principles of loyalty… of faithfulness… of honesty… is all that we should expect, and outside of that, there can really be no wrongdoing.

A woman who remains loyal and faithful to her incarcerated man is one hell of a woman, and I don't expect everyone to be capable of this kind of commitment. The relationship must be founded on something deeper than sex for it to work, and must truly care for their man's feelings and well-being. It's the same for the man as well… an incarcerated man who remains loyal and faithful to his woman is one hell of a man, and I DO expect every incarcerated man to be capable of this kind of commitment. He must remain conscious of her daily life and the problems she faces in the real world on a regular basis. Sometimes we forget that real life is stressful and that responsibility can be exhausting. We don't have any responsibilities in here, and our stress is of a different nature. We should always remember how blessed we are to have a good woman by our side, and never take her for granted. She does not have to be with you, and hopefully she's with you because she loves you for who you are. Don't get big headed and do anything stupid; be a good man, a man of integrity and sound principles, and TRUST your woman if you have one worthy of it. Really trust her and watch how happy it makes you.

Blog Post #5- August 6, 2021

What is MoreThanAnInmate?

MoreThanAnInmate is a way of life, an idea which has developed over the last few years as I have grown and changed as an incarcerated man.

Over the last decade I've had many moments when I'd lay here in bed at night, thinking "I could have did so much more with my life and been so much more as a man..." and it was during one of these moments of self-pity when I decided I STILL CAN do something special and express the potential that life offers all of us.

A man in my situation (serving a life sentence) has very limited choices, and many of the available options are "self-destructive" and are easy traps to fall into...which is the sad story of your average inmate. Many people give up and lose passion, lose their lust for life, and develop harmful habits. It has never been easy for anyone in history to overcome their oppression, and it has always been an ideal which requires hard work, discipline, persistence, self-confidence, belief, and risk...and may possibly end in failure...but, MoreThanAnInmate represents those who will make the attempt even when the odds are against them.

"Vision" is what guides an incarcerated person to becoming MoreThanAnInmate...dreams and goals, passions and desire, and the discipline required to work towards manifesting their reality. Vision is different than a "prison fantasy" or simple day dreaming; it is what allows us to approach each day with our head held high, giving our life a purpose worthy of pursuing.

MoreThanAnInmate is the confirmation that one holds on to while they are oppressed within these walls, something that one knows about themselves while looking in the mirror. It's the constant reminder that we will not let these people defeat us, and that we will fight, not with violence, but with KNOWLEDGE and COMMUNICATION. Through our way of living there will be no contradiction between our actions and our words, between our beliefs and our goals, between our desires and our happiness. We will remain balanced, understanding that the lower one digs the higher one climbs...as long as we continue to get up and proceed.

You have shown your support toward the incarcerated culture simply by reading my writings, but imagine how much good we could do in the world if we could work together under one platform and inspire change within this system. This is bigger than me, this is bigger than you, it's bigger than us. We must fight this system that continues to empower a caste system within our society.

People make mistakes--many of us have broken a law once or twice in our life time--and ties need to stop being severed between inmates and the community. In fact, we NEED the opposite--we need to build and strengthen ties between inmates and the community. Statistics show that inmates are more willing to change their behavior when they have some form of community support. Out of the 2.5 million incarcerated people in America, 90% of them feel "shunned" by our society, abandoned by their loved ones, and see no reason to change their ingrained habits. What incentive does one have to "rehabilitate" and change one's actions, to "become productive civilians", when they feel that the community they long to be a part of again is discriminatory against them? You can BE the support that someone may need; You may BE the reason for a change. A little bit of love can go a long ways...

Why is it your responsibility to show support for Prison Reform?--technically, it's not your responsibility at all! But, it only makes sense for one to appreciate a rehabilitated inmate as opposed to hardened, habitual criminals and right now our prisons generate the latter. What kind of people do you want leaving prison and re-entering society? Those who have received an education, and see the error of their ways? Or those who have spent years developing anti-social behavior and enhancing their criminal thought patterns?

I've seen both of these types, and what generally differentiates the two is that the rehabilitated had community support, while the habitual criminal has spent life feeling alone and neglected. MoreThanAnInmate defines all who see beyond the walls, who know that every life and every person are different, and who believe that there are many incarcerated people who deserve a second chance at life. But, I would never expect "blind faith" from anyone, would never "hope" that you automatically believe that there are incarcerated people that are more than simply "just an inmate"...thus, we are here to SHOW you the productivity and the rehabilitation, to SHARE with you the lives and the stories, the struggles and the triumphs, and to PROVIDE you with sufficient evidence that we hope would deter you from neglecting or discriminating against the inmate population as a whole.

Take the chance to get to know some of us. I'm not speaking for all of the inmate population...I can speak only for those who are MoreThanAnInmate, for those who want better for the world and better for themselves.

Show your support by adding us as a friend, or follow us to read new posts (hopefully sharing them with your friends and loved ones)

Have an amazing day!

Blog Post #6- August 10, 2021

What is "Felony Murder", and why must it be revised?

The "Felony Murder" rule is a theory which holds that if an *unplanned* murder occurs during the commission of a felony (such as robbery), all participants who are guilty of the "underlying felony" (robbery) thereby are guilty of First-degree Murder--EVEN IF THEY HAD NO PARTICIPATION IN THE MURDER ITSELF.

This rule has repetitively been used to sentence people to Life Without Parole--people who have never killed anybody nor assisted in the murder.

"It is a bedrock principle of the law and of equity that a person should be punished for his or her actions according to his or her own level of individual culpability." --quoted from California's Senate Bill #1437, which amended California's "felony murder rule"...to ensure that murder liability is not imposed on a person who is not the actual killer and did not act with the intent to kill.

In first-degree murder trials, the state must prove that a person "intended" to kill the victim. "Intent" is a material element that must be proven--that this person "intended" to kill somebody--in order to convict him/her of first-degree murder. This is true during all first-degree murder trials EXCEPT for when one is charged under the theory of "felony murder". In Nebraska, "felony murder" is a theory used to convict someone of first-degree murder, while eliminating any one's actual "intent to murder". An example of a felony murder case is when 3 people agree to rob a person, all agree to not harm any one, only one person is armed with a gun, and during the course of the robbery that one person shoots and kills the victim. Here, all 3 people will be charged with first-degree murder and given natural life sentences without the possibility of parole.

The "felony murder rule" allows for the state to convict somebody of first-degree murder EVEN THOUGH THEY NEVER POSSESSED THE INTENT TO KILL, nor did they "assist" with the murder. The rule states that if the participant is found to have had the "intent to commit robbery", then he/she is guilty of first-degree murder (in Nebraska).

A person who had no intent to harm anyone, let alone kill anyone, is convicted of the crime reserved for our society's most brutal and heinous murderers.

First-degree murder carries 2 choices of punishment which the judge is bound to impose upon the defendant: 1) a natural Life Sentence; OR, 2) the death penalty.

Do not mistake this post as me saying that I don't believe these 2 participants deserve to be punished--that's not what I'm saying at all. What I'm saying is that I believe the "felony murder rule" should either: be abolished; OR, *be charged as "second-degree murder"* (as opposed to first-degree). Second-degree murder carries a sentence any where between 20 years (minimum) and a Life sentence (maximum). So, 20 to Life, which would allow the judge to review each case on an individual basis, and sentence each offender to what the judge believes would be an appropriate punishment.

If felony murder was second-degree murder (as opposed to first-degree) the judge has the ability TO JUDGE each participant, sentencing them to their own level of culpability. For example: the actual shooter could receive 60-80 years and the 2 participants (who never killed anyone) could receive 40-50 years. This seems like a much more rational system of sentencing compared to forcing the judge to punish all 3 participants with natural life sentences--EVEN WHEN THE JUDGE OPENLY DECLARES HE/SHE DISAGREES WITH THE SENTENCE. Note that, if felony murder was second-degree murder, the judge is free to sentence each participant to a life sentence still--IF THEY BELIEVE THAT PUNISHMENT IS APPROPRIATE.

That is the major difference. *First-degree murder removes the judge's power to discriminate between each case on an individual basis-- discriminating being the purpose of a judge's position.* The "felony murder rule" falls under first-degree murder, which simply imposes the "intent to murder" upon somebody who never possessed the intent to harm, nor possessed any malice. It should be ruled "unconstitutional" for this rule to be tried as a first-degree murder case. It makes no sense, and it is Time for a Change!

#AbolishFelonyMurder!

Blog Post #7- August 19, 2021

I've had a lot of things on my mind lately, things I try to ignore and act like they don't bother me...but sometimes they do. Just with people around here, and the changes I've been making within my daily life and routine. The "changes" alone is one thing to deal with, but people I would like to consider my friends aren't necessarily supportive of my changes and I feel them starting to change on me as well. I've always known that if I ever gave up my previous lifestyle that 95% of the people that used to come around would immediately disappear, and I'm okay with that. But I sincerely was hoping that a few guys I've became close to over the years would let me "break away" without any hard feelings. The reality is that I truly have nothing in common with the people around me, besides the activities that I spent my entire prison sentence indulging in and becoming known for. Now that I'm dropping the common denominator people are acting like we don't know each other...and I guess that is the cold truth. We don't know each other. We never were "friends" who shared a history; we were associates who shared similar interests. I shouldn't expect anything more from them, as I would have done the same thing had things been the other way.

Many people don't want to see you do something better for yourself, and that is part of the problem. Something within them would rather hold you down rather than join the climb. Now when I hear conversations regarding the things and ideas that used to be the center of my life, things which used to be my drive, I almost become sick that this is what people waste their lives trying to accomplish, and it becomes clear to me how lost I was in the lifestyle--a lifestyle I am much better than, a lifestyle that we as a people are much better than. I'm on the outside looking in right now and I've never been able to see it more clearly. If we could only place this much of our energy and focus into productive activity rather than destructive activity we would rise high into the sky, no limit above us. Instead, we know what we're doing is morally wrong, effecting the way we see ourselves and the way we view others, but we are lost in our "convictions", truly believing this is meant for us. And this is where my associates have decided to rest, where they have convinced themselves that this is what life is and that they have no other options. And this is where I have decided to stand, to continue my journey forward, knowing there is much more to life than this and that there are better ways of receiving life's pleasantries.

There is no compromise between food and poison...death will always win. We have to eliminate the poison completely, which means that true change will require a complete break away from one's past, leaving it all behind, including the people. It's sad and it's hard, but how badly do you want better for yourself and your family? How different do you want your future to be? If you want to be better than your past, then your past is exactly what you may just have to let go of.

"You know what's been holding me back?...everyone that I wanted to take with me."

Blog Post #8- September 28, 2021

Somebody asked me the other day, "What do you mean when you say that you're a prison reformer?"

I figure that's a pretty good question worthy of spending some time to answer for every body. What is Prison Reform?

Mass incarceration of human beings within America has become a serious problem, one which it is pretty clear where the mistakes lie.

You will hear me repeat the statistics of America's inmate population compared to the world's (20-25% of the planet's inmates) regularly because I want it to soak into the subconscious mind of citizens. America has 3% of the world's population--ideally we should have around 3% of the world's inmates--ESSENTIALLY because our crime rate IS NOT substantially higher than that of other countries. Contrary to what the media wants us to believe, America does NOT have a crime "problem". Yes, we have crime--all countries have (and always will have) but not a problem worthy of mass incarceration at this rate.

"Prison Reform" is *any work done which can assist the process of lowering America's incarceration numbers dramatically.* We, as a country, have a "mass incarceration" problem--NOT a crime problem. My ideal of a finished reformation of America's prison system is to see a decrease in the statistic from 25% down to 5%. This means a shift from 2.5 million inmates to 500,000 incarcerated humans. Yes, this would mean a mass "release" of people, as well as several changes within the established policies and procedures that are currently in place.

My ideas of prison reform require the abolishment of:

*Mandatory Minimum prison sentences

*the Death Penalty across all states

*Life Sentences that do not have the possibility of parole

*the "felony murder" rule

*Private-owned prisons "for profit"

*the abuse of segregation/isolation as punishment

*prosecutorial "quid pro quo" with State witnesses

My ideas also require us to revise certain policies and procedures, such as providing:

*"compassionate release" for elderly inmates (over 65) who qualify for release (non-threat)

*early release of all "non-violent inmates"

*rehabilitation & education facilities, instead of warehouse & storage buildings

*proper training of correctional officers, to treat inmates as humans, as opposed to animals

*"electric ankle monitors" instead of new prisons

*"work release opportunities" instead of warehouses

*"compassionate considerations" towards juvenile offenders

Further, I believe we should:

*"de-fund prisons", spending the funds on rehabilitation centers instead

*decriminalize drug use & prostitution (as these crimes have no specific victim)

*develop more "non-profit organizations" for our troubled youth to participate in *bring awareness to the "New Jim Crow" system implemented within our country as mass incarceration and felon stamps

Each one of these "revisions" can be briefly described and compared to other country's statistics, who see that rehabilitation of a prisoner is more sufficient to their society "as a whole"--as opposed to creating, then releasing, "hardened criminals" back into a world that legally discriminates against them, and expects them not to re-offend.

As a "prison reformer", the goal of my work--as well as the meaning of my life--is *to decrease the prison population and to change current policies that allow this cycle to continue*. Many things within our country, as well as other countries, deserve to be looked at and re-established--prison reformation is simply the one I feel closest too as I am currently suffering from these inhumane policies. A man like myself, who never killed or harmed any body and never possessed any intent to kill or harm any body, is serving a Life sentence without the possibility of parole, sentenced at the age of 20 to die "by old age" within these prison walls-- and I have harmed no one physically. I do not believe this to be justice, and is simply *one flaw* within our system.

Change begins with awareness--awareness comes from discussion and expression. My battle begins here with this chosen platform of Facebook. I've been incarcerated for 12 years (all of my adult life) and I know nothing as of how to utilize social media and have no knowledge as to how things on the internet actually work. I'm an alien to this culture, but I will continue to write my thoughts and ideas, my lady will continue to post them for me, and we will continue to bring awareness to the fact that good people are trapped behind prison bars due to unjust policies & procedures and/or lifestyles that are contradictive to the ideals of an American society.

Reach out to us and assist with this battle!

A special thanks to all of those who are currently fighting this battle on their own terms and through their own methods. You are highly appreciated! We need a group of "united individuals" against mass incarceration. I'll be here to show the world that some of us are More Than An Inmate.

Please share any opinions/ideas that you may see fit for prison reformation, and if you disagree with any of my ideas please share your thoughts with me in a constructive criticism manner. I'm open minded and would love to learn from other people's views and ways of life.

I'd like to end with a sincere apology to any/all who have been hurt or effected by crime within our country. I am sorry for your loss and your pain and I mean to take nothing away from the victims within our country. Justice must be served, and I pray you find within your heart peace & healing, forgiveness, understanding, and personal security.

Let's stop this cycle of pain, suffering, and hurt by reforming a prison system, rehabilitating those who are about to come home, who truly need to be educated and assisted before being released back into society.

#MoreThanAnInmate

Blog Post #9- October 1, 2021

Lately I've been reading about different cultures and their struggles, truly been trying to "see" the inequalities within our society. As I am "white" and I am a "man" sometimes it's easy for me to ignore certain privileges that I may have had, and it's taken for me to truly remove myself from myself in order to view the world objectively. Erase all of the bias that I inherently possess, as we all do, and truly look at the world for what it is. It is not simple to see the world from outside of ourselves, but the "attempt" to do so is the requirement of our metropolitan society. I finished reading a book called "The New Jim Crow: Mass Incarcerating in the Age of Colorblindness"--which helped me understand the answer to "why" our prisons do not "rehabilitate" people. It helped me grasp how deep "hate & discrimination" lie within the body of our society, the core of its sole.

Jim Crow laws were the laws of "segregation" after the end of slavery. From the end of slavery til the Civil Rights movement of the 60's, laws allowed for racial segregation.

The end of Jim Crow and segregation was celebrated by the masses as a step toward the end of a "racist society". But, rather than eliminating "racism & legal discrimination", *a new Jim Crow system was born*, one which is disguised and labeled as "colorblind" --the mass incarceration. America's crisis. In the early 90's, America housed around 300,000 inmates within their entire prison population. Within 30 years the inmate population has dramatically increased to 2.5 million people! This means the entire prison population increased by 100,000 inmates per year!

During the era of Jim Crow, it was the black race that people shunned and were trying to distinguish themselves from. The inherent need to "distinguish" one's self from a different class of people, the thought that "I can't be associated with THEM". The need to feel that you are better than a different class of people--this ugly instinct has now been shifted and placed upon the inmate population. People fear being associated with the prison reform movement as "it is beneath them and their peers" (i.e. social suicide).

The label of "felon" is the tool that America has used to sustain its caste system--not a "class", but a "caste". Being branded as a felon bars one from mainstream society and the business economy, and people are legally allowed to treat a felon as less than a civilian. Today, it is no longer a question of race because the New Jim Crow is "colorblind"--allowing people to reinforce morals and beliefs, rationalizing with themselves that felons have "made the choice to break the law" which places them "beneath" those who have not committed a crime. Because some broke "the law" (which, keep in mind, is a MAN-MADE creation of rules & regulations set in place deliberately to benefit those who created it) a stamp is placed upon them, labeled as a "felon", thus, are now legally segregated from the realm of equal opportunity; are now "beneath" the natural rights of Life, Liberty, and the pursuit of Happiness.

On paper, this system is "colorblind" simply because the prisons are filled with people of all races, nationalities, and cultures--but, beneath this disguise, this system was developed for the purpose and with the intent to confine and segregate the black race. Any one who falls into this "trap" set in place for the African Americans and other minorities are wrote off as "collateral damage", and are of no loss to our society. Simply witness how a family who comes from wealth, they may break the same laws but suffer none of the consequences that the poverty class will suffer if the roles were reversed.

The laws put in place are ones which the system knows there is a 33% chance of all African Americans breaking at one point in their lives, thus, legally becoming segregated again--this time disguised as having made their own conscious choice to become segregated. The large amounts of "collateral damage" (poor white people) who have fallen into these traps are simply statistics on paper utilized by politicians to hide their racist agenda and cover up this New Jim Crow segregation scheme.

Law is nothing but a trap.

Millions of people who have never harmed a person and have never infringed upon the freedoms of another are "segregated", placed outside of society's boundaries, reserved as "last resorts" and for the jobs of hard, physical labor.

What does that sound like to you?

Millions of people's lives have been ruined by simply possessing a large amount of marijuana--but then major companies are allowed to sell large amounts of marijuana?

Punishment is okay. People need to learn and understand the responsibility that freedom entails, and they need to be punished for infringing upon the freedoms of others.

BUT--a "caste system" should not be accepted by any citizen who claims to be a person of morals, of religion, of philosophy. No body should be forced into a "caste system"; it must not be acceptable in what we call the most free country in the world.

America should not be housing 25% of the global inmate population when our country only claims 3% of the entire human population.

This mass incarceration is outrageous!

Any one who fears to have any affiliation with the inmate community, for any reason--you are today's version of the people from a century ago who oppressed and segregated the black race. Look in the mirror and understand that because of "social grace" you ignore the segregation taking place in front of you. *"Prison Reform" is a moral duty of every American,* and one should openly associate and accept those who show themselves to be More Than An Inmate.

What distinguishes America's mass incarceration from that of the Holocaust is the term "colorblind" and the fact that they are not murdering and torturing us within these walls. But, they are effectively ridding society of a group whom they do not want to procreate and have successful children.

A woman becomes a "felon" in an attempt to defend her children from violence. Ignorant of the law and equipped with an ineffective "state-provided" attorney, she "plead guilty" to this felony charge and was sentenced to one-year of probation. That was 15-years ago and she still suffers to this day from the discrimination of possessing the "felony" label. This woman will never be seen as a hard-working, independent woman-- she will be seen as a "felon" (i.e. trouble).

This is not acceptable within our country. European countries (Great Britain & Scandanavia) have no such label that allows one to legally discriminate against their citizens; they have no "caste system" as we do in America.

Understand what is taking place.

Although I don't necessarily agree with or support the "means" by which some people would like to see a change, I highly recommend reading "The New Jim Crow" as literature that can open ones eyes to what this mass incarceration and the "felon caste system" is doing to our society. #MoreThanAnInmate

<u>Blog Post #10- June 26, 2024</u>

It's been awhile since I posted on here. A couple years, actually, and a lot has happened since then. I'm sure a lot has happened in each of your own lives as well...hopefully nothing but positivity, growth, success, happiness, and love...but how rare is that? Most of us are probably "just okay", still pushing through our daily lives and struggling with this new economy. It's been different, hasn't it? And it feels like things keep changing but aren't really leading us anywhere out of the turmoil.

We all have our inner turmoil within our lives. At the heart of mine..it's always been dealing with this judicial system. Always has been, probably always will be. Since the time of my last post, I've lost all of my appeals. Just received a letter this morning actually, stating the 8thCircuit won't even review my case. But why am I not surprised? We all know by now this system isn't meant for justice...this is nothing new. Millions before me have suffered this same fate.

But as one door closes, another one opens. I have no appeals, all of my ships have been burned, and nothing is left but to face my reality...one that appears dark and bleak. But within this darkness, I've discovered a new energy inside my soul that is determined to fight for my survival. It's either fight or die in here for me, there is no longer the flight option...but surprisingly, I feel more hopeful than I ever have, more optimistic than I've ever been. My future seems more bright than I've ever imagined.

I no longer have a choice in the matter of what I "must do" and tunnel vision has enveloped my senses. I'd never truly experienced tunnel vision until these moments, until these last couple of weeks, and it's made me feel more alive than I've ever felt. I feel closer to my freedom now than I ever have throughout this incarceration...and it's because now I know. There's no more guessing or wondering, I have my answers. *These people are not going to let me out of here.* They're just not.

Does this mean I should give up? Does this serve as an excuse for me to willow in my misery? Absolutely not. This gives me reason, this gives me motivation and inspiration, to put my all into what I've always believed but now KNOW is my life's purpose. Every morning I wake up at 5am excited about getting to work, excited like a kid waking up on Christmas. I'm excited to unleash upon the world the VOICE of inmates who have been oppressed too long, silenced by the system. I'm excited to play my part in introducing to the world those who are More Than An Inmate. I'm excited about disrupting the status quo of America's mass incarceration beliefs. I'm excited by life, in general. For even though I am still serving a Life sentence in Nebraska's maximum-security prison...I am happy. I am grateful for all that I have, thankful for everything I've been through and experienced. It's time to work.

"They tried to bury us.

They didn't know we were seeds."

Sit back and watch us blossom.

#freeNicholasEly

…Interested in reading more blog posts?

Have your friends and family follow my facebook blog "More Than an

Inmate" by going to facebook.com/freenicholasely. I've been posting

about twice a week since June 26 2024.

APPENDIX

Cheat Sheet

<u>Prisoner Principles</u>

1) No snitchin

2) No stealing

3) Mind Your Own Business

4) Pay Your Bills

5) Respect people's space

6) Don't call people out of their name

<u>12 Virtues</u>

1) Reliability

2) Humility

3) Prudence

4) Fortitude

5) Resilience

6) Patience

7) Studiousness

8)Temperance

9)Justice

10) Gratitude

<u>12 Vices</u>

1) Resentment

2) Complacency

3) Stupidity

4) Avarice

5) Rashness

6) Solipsism

7) Wantonness

8) Indolence

9) Lack of Perspective

10) Despair

11) Progress

12) Tranquility

11) Self-Deceit

12) Addiction

<u>12 Principles to obtain Wisdom</u>

1) Take care of yourself - physically, emotionally, spiritually

2) Live your life out of Vision, not out of circumstance

3) Develop a strong bullshit detector.

4) Don't let your ego fool you

5) Be reticent in public.

6) Focus on Healing, NOT on what is divisive

7) Work regularly to increase your will power

8) React prudently to the vicissitudes of life

9) Treat cheating like it's treason

10) Don't let customs or tradition overrule your good sense

11). Always remind children of their importance to society

12) Be the change you want to see in the world

<u>Agents of Change must:</u>

1) Alter the way you see your time.

2) Create a routine that pushes you towards your goals AND STICK TO

   IT!

3) Educate yourself

4) Network, and respect boundaries

5) Enlighten

Resources

For Business:

www.legalzoom.com (incorporate your business)

www.corporatedirect.com (incorporate your business).

www.hyperurl.co/ein (EIN registration)

www.yelp.com (claim your brand)

www.wikipedia.com (claim your brand)

www.marketing-mentos.com (helps small businesses market)

www.sba.gov (assistance to small businesses)

Grammarly for Business (sound professional when you write)

www.uline.com (sells office and business supplies)

www.theliquidator.com (online liquidation auctions)

www.4imprints.com (place logo on merchandise)

www.vistaprint.com (business cards, greeting cards, etc.)

www. affiliate-program.amazon.com (link your site to Amazon)

www.merch.amazon.com (sell t-shirts on Amazon)

www.ups.com (business assistance)

www.fedex.com (business assistance)

Make your website:

www.wordpress.org

www.godaddy.com/airo

Shopify

List all your profiles together:

www.about.me

www.vizify.com

Turn email into a signature:

www.airtimehg.com

Search a topic:

www.findarticles.com

Find lost money

www.unclaimedproperty.com

www.missingmoney.com

Compile Statistics

www.statbrain.com

Capture Emails

www.mailchimp.com

The Global Media Center for Social Impact:

www.cinemaofchange.com/directory/listing/the-ghbal-mediu-center-for-social-impact

Print On Demand clothing /accessory:

Printify

Printful

Society6

Zazzle

For Writers:

www.copyright.gov

www.myidentifiers.org

www.bowker.com (purchase ISBN numbers)

www.copytheformula.com (a format)

penonfire.com (an editor)

www.loc.gov (Library of Congress - donate books as tax deductions)

www.masterclass.com (instructions from author Dan Brown)

Print On Demand self-publishing -

Amazon KDP

LuLu

Create Space

Lightning Print

Book Baby

Ingram Spark

<u>Sites that will publish writings of prisoners:</u>

www.writersdigest.com

www.prisonjournalismproject.org

www.allrise.media.org

www.betweenthebars.org

www.jpp.org (journal of prisoners)

www.the marshallproject.org (prison watch dogs)

www.pen.org/prison-writing

www.prisonwriters.com

www.prisonerexpress.org

www.prisonsfoundation.org

www.solitarywatch.org

www.undergroundwriting.org

www.thesunmagazine.org

<u>Useful Apps (tools):</u>

Fiverr (freelancers)

Chat GPT. (generates writing and images)

Claude

Gemini

Handwriting-to-Text Recognition

Canva (graphic design)

PicsArt (graphic design)

Capcut (video editing)

Recommended Reading

<u>Self-Help</u>

"The Daily Laws" by Robert Greene

"The 7 Habits of Highly Effective People" by Stephen Covey

"Think And Grow Rich" by Napolean Hill

"The Four Agreements" by Don Miguel Ruiz

"Man's Search for Meaning" by Victor Frankl

"How Successful People Think" by John Maxwell

<u>Healing</u>

"Waking the tiger: Healing Trauma" by Peter E. Levine

"In An Unspoken Voice" by Peter A. Levine (trauma)

"Non Violent Communication: Healthy Relationships" by Marshall Rosenberg

"The Myth of Normal" by Gabor Mate

"Self Therapy" by Jay Earley

<u>Psychology</u>

"Mind War" by Michael Aquino

"ADHD and the Edison Gene" by Thomas Hartmann

"The Laws of Human Nature" by Robert Greene

"The 48 Laws of Power" by Robert Greene

"Create Your Own Religion" by Daniele Balleli

"12 Rules for Life" by Jordan Peterson

<u>Seduction</u>

"The Game" by Neil Strauss

"The 5 Love Languages" by Gary Chapman

"Men are from Mars, Women are from Venus" by John Gray

"The Art of Seduction" by Robert Greene

"Love and Respect" by Emerson Eggerichs

<u>Incarceration</u>

"Solitary" by Albert Woodfox

"The New Jim Crow" by Michelle Alexander

"Miller's Children" by James Garbarino

<u>Business</u>

"Rich Dad Poor Dad" (trilogy series) by Robert Kiyosaki

"Start Your Own Corporation" by Garrett Sutton

"Writing Winning Business Plans" by Garrett Sutton

"Finance Your Own Business" by Garrett Sutton.

"The Richest Man in Babylon" by George S. Clason

"Capitalism: The Unknown Ideal" by Ayn Rand

<u>Real Estate</u>

"The ABC's of Real Estate Investing" by Ken McElroy

"Beginners Guide to Real Estate Investing" by Gary Eldred

"How to Invest in Debt" by Michael Pellegrino

<u>Writing</u>

"Jailhouse Publishing" by Mike Enemigo

"The Sentences that Create Us" by Caits Meissner, a PEN America Book

<u>Resourceful</u>

The World Almanac (most recent year, it's our "google")

American Heritage dictionary (or any dictionary, but must have one)

Prisoners Self Help Litigation Manual

The Jailhouse Lawyer's Handbook

Wellness Toolkits

Provided by:

National Institutes of Health.

www.nih.gov/wellnessted Kits

<u>Emotional Wellness Checklist</u>

Emotional wellness is the ability to successfully handle life's stresses and adapt to change and difficult times. Here are tips for improving your emotional health:

- Brighten Your Outlook. People who are emotionally well, experts say, have fewer negative emotions and are able to bounce back from difficulties faster.
- This quality is called resilience. Another sign of emotional wellness is being able to hold onto positive emotions longer and appreciate the good times.
    - o To develop a more positive mindset:
        - Remember your good deeds.
        - Forgive yourself.
        - Spend more time with your friends.

- Explore your beliefs about the meaning and purpose of life.

- Develop healthy physical habits.

- Reduce Stress. Everyone feels stressed from time to time. Stress can give you a rush of energy when it's needed most. But if stress lasts a long time - a condition known as chronic stress - those "high alert" changes become harmful rather than helpful. Learning healthy ways to cope with stress can boost your resilience.

  o To help manage your stress:

    - Get enough sleep

    - Exercise regularly

    - Build a social support network

    - Set priorities

    - Think positive

    - Try relaxation methods

    - Seek help

- Get Quality Sleep. To fit in everything we want to do in our day, we often sacrifice sleep. But sleep affects both mental and physical health. It's vital to your well-being. When you're tired, you can't function at your best. Sleep helps you think more clearly, have quicker reflexes and forms better. Take steps to make sure you regularly get a good night's sleep.

- o   To get a better quality sleep:

  - Go to bed and get up each day at the same time

  - Sleep in a dark, quiet place

  - Exercise daily

  - Limit the use of electronics

  - Relax before bedtime

  - Avoid alcohol, nicotine, and stimulants late in the day

  - Consult a health care professional if you have ongoing sleep problems

- Be Mindful. The concept of mindfulness is simple. This ancient practice is about being completely aware of what's happening in the present - of all going on inside and all that's happening around you. It means not living your life on autopilot. Becoming a more mindful person requires commitment and practice.

  - o   To be more mindful:

    - Take some deep breaths through your nose to a count of 4, hold for 1 Second and then exhale through the mouth to a count of 5. Repeat often.

    - Enjoy a stroll and notice the sights around you.

    - Practice mindful eating. Be aware of each bite and when you're full.

- Find mindfulness resources in your local community, including classes, programs, or books.

- Cope With Loss. When someone you love dies, your world changes. There is no right or wrong way to mourn. Although the death of a loved one can feel overwhelming, people can make it through the grieving process with the support of family and friends. Learn healthy ways to help you through difficult times.

  o To help cope with loss;

    - Take care of yourself

    - Talk to a caring friend

    - Try not to make any major changes right away

    - Join a grief support group

    - Consider professional support

    - Talk to your doctor if you're having trouble with everyday activities

    - Be patient. Mourning takes time

- Strengthen Social Connections. Social connections might help protect health and lengthen life. Scientists are finding that our links to others can have powerful effects on our health - both emotionally and physically. Whether with romantic partners, family, friends, neighbors, or others, social connections can influence our biology and well-being.

- o   To build healthy support systems:

    - Build strong relationships with your kids.

    - Get active and share good habits with family and friends.

    - If you're a family caregiver, ask for help from others.

    - Join a group focused on a favorite hobby, such as reading, hiking, or painting.

    - Take a class to learn something new.

    - Volunteer for things you care about in your community, like a community garden, school, library, or place of worship.

    - Travel to different places and meet new people.

<u>Social Wellness Checklist</u>

Positive social habits can help you build support systems and stay healthier mentally and physically. Here are some tips for connecting with others:

-   Build Healthy Relationships. Strong, healthy relationships are important throughout your life. They can impact your mental and physical well-being. As a child you learn the social skills you need to form and maintain relationships with others. But at any age you can learn ways to improve your relationships. It is important to know what a healthy relationship looks like and how to keep your connections supportive.

- o   To Build healthy relationships:

    - Share your feelings honestly.

    - Ask for what you need from others.

    - Listen to others without judgment or blame. Be caring and empathetic

    - Disagree with others respectfully. Conflicts should not turn into personal attacks.

    - Avoid being overly critical, angry outbursts, and violent behavior.

    - Expect others to treat you with respect and honesty in return.

    - Compromise. Try to come to agreements that work for everyone.

    - Protect yourself from violent and abusive people. Set boundaries with others.

    - Decide what you are and aren't willing to do. It's okay to say no.

- Learn the differences between healthy, unhealthy, and abusive ways of relating to others. Visit https://www.thehotline.org/resources/healthy-relationships/

<u>Physical Wellness Checklist</u>

Positive physical habits can decrease your stress, lower your risk of disease, and increase your energy. Here are tips for improving your physical health:

- Get Active. How well your body functions affects your ability to accomplish your daily activities. Sedentary behavior - which usually means sitting or lying down while awake - has been linked to a shorter lifespan and a wide range of medical problems. Any time you get up and move, you're improving your chances for good health.
  - o To increase your activity:
    - Take the stairs instead of the elevator
    - Have walking meetings with colleagues.
    - Walk on a treadmill while watching TV or using the computer.

- Set an alarm on your computer to go off every hour and prompt you to move around for a minute or two.

- Try walking as if you're already late.

- Have small weights in your office or home.

- Maintain Your Body. Your bones, muscles, and joints all work together to make your body an amazing movable machine. Like any machine, your body can suffer some wear and tear. It needs regular care and maintenance to keep moving with ease.

  o To keep your body healthier:

    - Maintain a healthy weight.

    - Engage in muscle strengthening activities.

    - Aim for 150 minutes of moderate intensity activity each week.

    - Wear comfortable, properly fitting shoes.

    - Eat a well-balanced diet

    - Try to avoid lifting heavy objects.

- Eat a healthy Diet. We make dozens of decisions every day. When it comes to deciding what to eat and feed our families, it can be a lot easier than one might think to make smart choices. A healthy eating plan not only limits unhealthy foods, but also includes a variety of healthy foods.

- To eat a healthier diet:

    - Replace saturated fats, like butter or meat fat, with unsaturated fats, like vegetable oil.

    - Cut back on sodium. Choose fresh foods and those that have no added salt or less than 5% of the Daily Value of sodium per serving.

    - Choose more complex carbs, like whole grain breads, cereals, starchy vegetables, and legumes.

    - Cut added sugars, Pick food with little or no added sugar

    - Get more fiber. Switch to whole grains and eat more vegetables, beans, nuts, and seeds.

- Mind Your Metabolism. Your metabolism changes as you get older. You burn fewer calories and break down foods differently. You also lose lean muscle. Unless you exercise more and adjust your diet, the pounds can add up. Middle-age spread can quickly become middle-age sprawl. Carrying those extra pounds may be harming your health.

    - To combat age-related changes:

        - Commit to a healthy diet

        - Limit snacking

        - Drink plenty of water.

- Move more. Take the stairs and add walking breaks to you day

- Get plenty of sleep.

- Limit alcohol use.

- Avoid tobacco products. When you quit smoking, you may improve many aspects of your health and are likely to add years to your life.

- Build Healthy Habits. We knew that making healthy choices can help us feel better and live longer. Maybe you've already tried to eat better, get more exercise for sleep, quit smoking, er reduce stress. It's not easy. But research shows how you can boost your ability to create and sustain a healthy lifestyle.

  o To build healthy habits:

    - Plan. Set realistic goals.

    - Change your surroundings. Remove temptations.

    - Ask for support.

    - Fill your time with healthy activities.

    - Track your progress.

    - Imagine the future.

    - Reward yourself.

    - Be patient. Improvement takes time, and setbacks happen. Focus on progress, not perfection.

- Find a Healthy Weight. Keeping your body at a healthy weight may help your risk of heart disease, type 2 diabetes, and certain types of cancer that can result from being overweight or obese. Take charge of your weight and your health.

    o To reach your weight loss goals:

        - Eat smaller portions.

        - Eat colorful vegetables each day.

        - Choose whole grains.

        - Go easy on sugar, fats, and oils.

        - Stick with activities you enjoy.

        - Go for a brisk walk, ride a bike, or do some gardening

        - Do strengthening activities.

        - Get active for just 10 minutes, several times a day. Each little bit counts!

        - Keep a food and physical activity diary.

        - Be realistic and aim for slow, modest weight loss.

About the Author

Nicholas J. Ely *was born on August 31st, 1990, in Des Moines, Iowa.*

Raised in Sioux City, Iowa, by divorced parents, he was 15 when he was

locked up for the first time. Released at 17 years old, he later lived in

Omaha, Nebraska, where he graduated from Northwest High School.

By profession, Nicholas is an author who writes books for incarcerated

people;

By captivity, a prisoner serving a natural life sentence (since 2011) for a

"felony murder" conviction; and, by hustle, a baker of cheesecakes and

maker of hot pockets that feed the prisoner's soul.

Having only been free for eighteen months since the age of 15, Nicholas

has not experienced the world since he was 20 years old. He hopes that one day the system will acknowledge the science of brain development and forgive him for the impulsive, desperate, and youthful decisions he made.

With no violence on his institutional record, Nicholas has still spent four years in solitary confinement and four years in a supermax controlled movement unit. Fortunately, this isolation provided nearly a decade of reflection, reading, and personal growth, ultimately transforming him into a different person—a better person.

Intrigued by philosophy and religion, you will often find Nicholas with his nose in a book that requires a dictionary to understand. After becoming an advocate himself, Nicholas aspires to educate and provide a voice for other incarcerated individuals. He writes and posts blogs regularly at Facebook.com/freenicholasely and works to "End the Felony Murder Rule in Nebraska."

Nicholas has dreams and high hopes that one day he will be free again with his wife, family, and loved ones. For now, his reality is spending 21 hours a day in a cell by himself—reading, writing, exercising, and planning his next move in the fight for justice.

Follow the author on social media:

Instagram: More Than An Inmate

Facebook: More Than An Inmate

TikTok: @freenicholasely

Website: www.morethananinmate.com

You can write the author by mailing a letter to:

More Than an Inmate

13310 NE 177th Pl

Ste B101 #3090

Woodinville, WA 98072

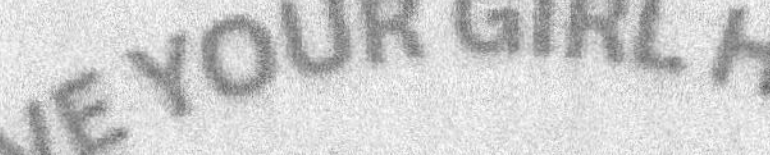

Tell your people –
this is the one they need to hear.

"For every woman holding
it down – this one's for you".

More Than an
Inmate's Girlfriend
PODCAST

Listen on

 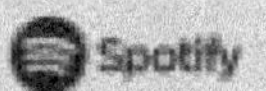 Spotify  amazon music

iHeartRADIO

Instagram: @podcast_prisongf
TikTok: @morethananinmatesgf

A Catalog for Incarcerated Men to Send Gifts to
Their Loved Ones at Home

Show her you love her—
even from the inside

✓ Strengthen your relationship

✓ Send meaningful gifts

✓ Make her feel appreciated

Books Published By
BestSelf Publications

Available on Amazon, Barned&Noble and www.bestselfpublications.com

"The Prisoner's Manifesto" by Nicholas J. Ely defines how to live a life of integrity and morals while being incarcerated.

"Reform Starts With Us" By Nicholas J. Ely is a declaration that reform won't come until we realize that it starts with us, the people incarcerated, and who we need to become if we want to be accepted again.

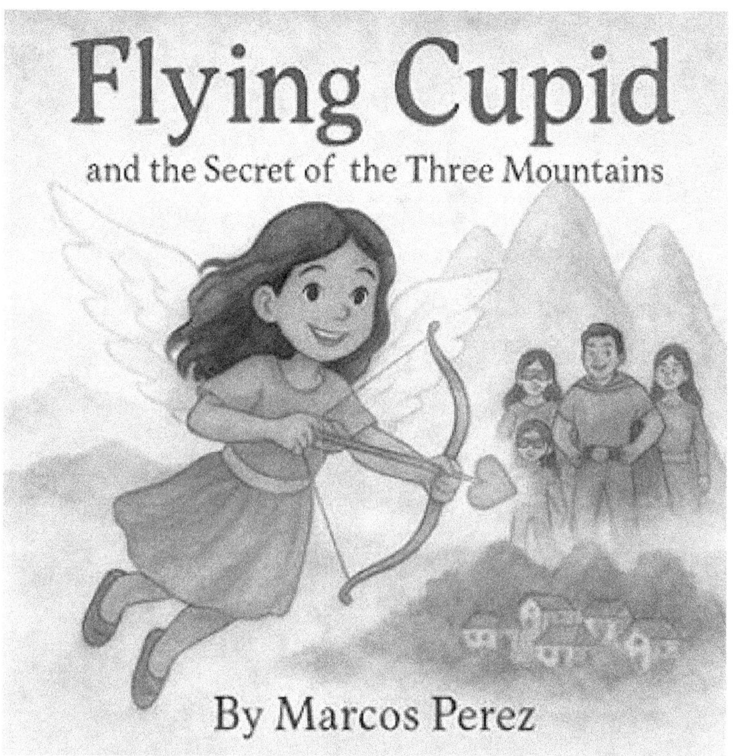

Children's book "Flying Cupid and The Secret of the Three Mountains"
By Marcos Perez
A Young girl's journey to turning a vampire back into her dad

"The Enochian Bible" by Ysl Enochial. Enoch has verified this truth, and teaches us that we must not follow the disturbed organizations called churches, or place our faith within corrupt corporations that drain man of his potential life energy

"The Testament of Enoch" is a pocketbook companion to the Enochian Bible.

Reflecting Upon Life *A journal prompt a day (with the page to write out) for a year to document your life and reflections while being incarcerated*

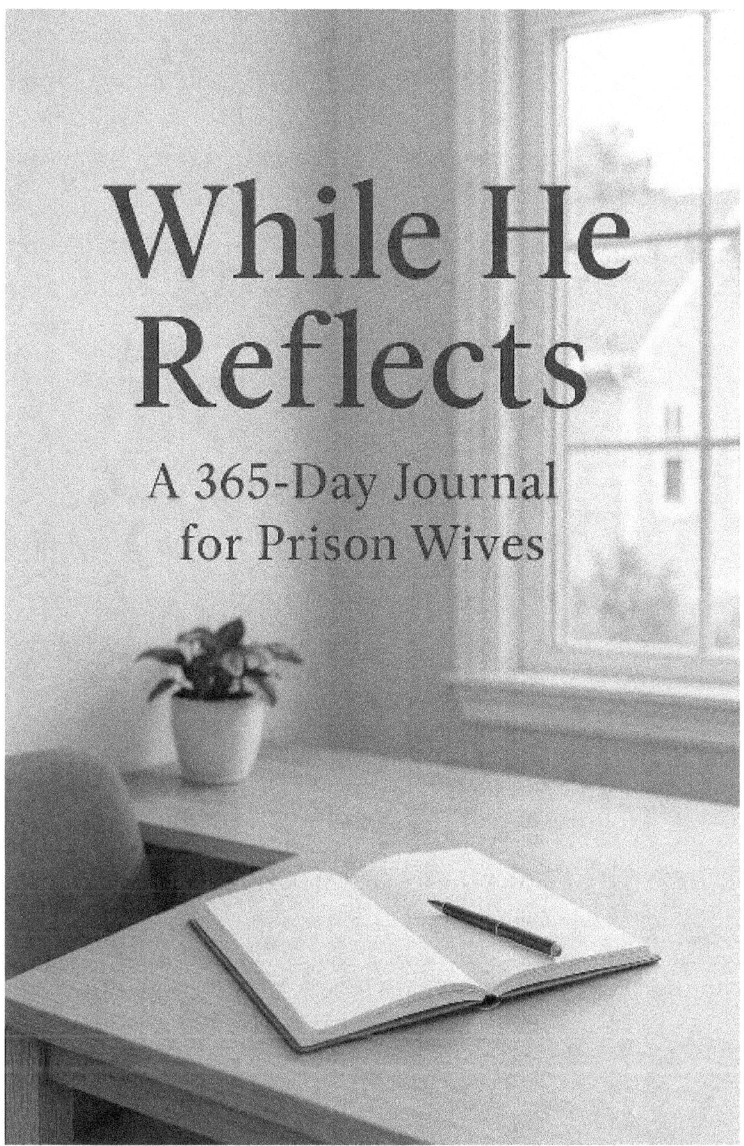

"While He Reflects.. a 365 day journal for prison wives" is the counterpart of Reflecting Upon Life for the prison wife to document her journey that got her here while he does the same in prison

The Best Prisoner's Cookbook Ever Published!

Does it need another explanation? Microwave preferable for most recipes

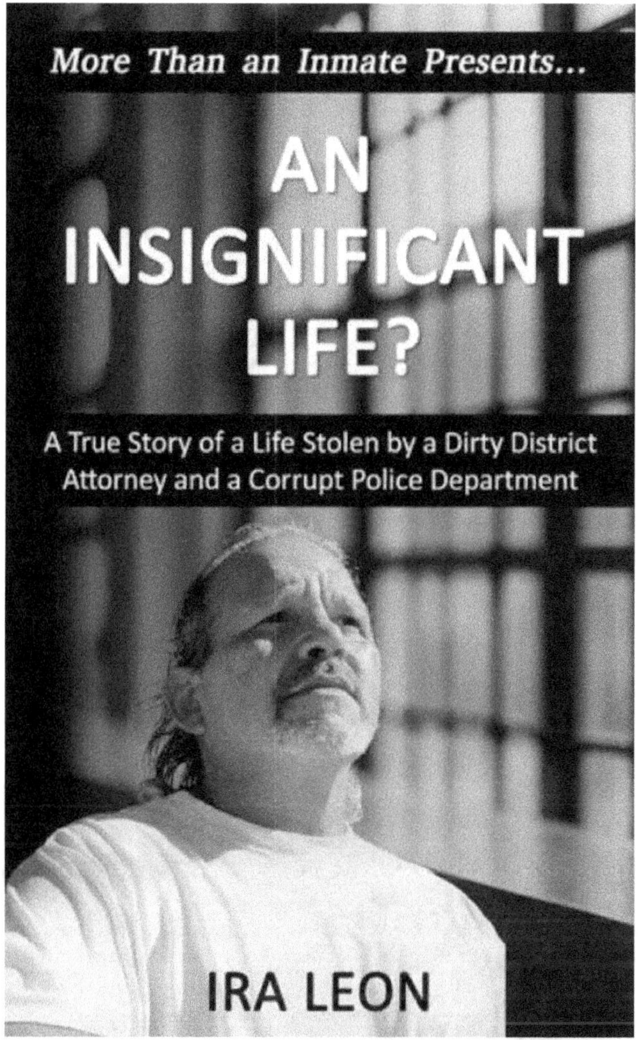

"An Insignificant Life?" by Ira Leon is the story of how Ira was incarcerated in 1992 under the felony murder rule for a murder he did not commit... and everyone knows it.

A collection of poems and art collected from incarcerated individuals as well as some examples of misconduct reports handed out over the years.

"ATL Above The Law" by TJ Foster is an urban novel based in Detroit where the King of the streets has been indicted and now there's room for others to come in..

A serial killer on the loose in Michigan. A former marine's wife goes missing and the captor leaves one word behind: Obsessed. Will they find her in time?

Money, power, and destruction collide when a home invasion turns deadly, forever altering countless lives. In Detroit's dangerous underworld, Grip and his crew risk everything for wealth, fame, and survival.

From the trenches to the elite, Detroit erupts in scandal as newly elected mayor Quincy Pope fights to protect his secrets. When a councilman threatens to expose him, political chaos could destroy everything he's built